# THE MAKING OF
# RAGING BULL

D1188798

# THE MAKING OF
# RAGING BULL

**MIKE EVANS**

The publisher wishes to thank the Book Division at Lasgo Chrysalis London
for their ongoing support in developing this series.

Published by Unanimous Ltd.
Unanimous Ltd. is an imprint of MQ Publications Ltd.
12 The Ivories, 6–8 Northampton Street, London, N1 2HY

Printed and bound in France

ISBN: 1-903318-83-1

1 2 3 4 5 6 7 8 9

# contents

# introduction

One of the few films from the Eighties to regularly appear in the Top Ten lists of both audiences and critics, *Raging Bull's* reputation has grown over the years to the point where it is now rightly considered an all-time classic.

A "difficult" film by any standards, its uncompromising treatment of boxer Jake La Motta's harrowing autobiography won instant critical acclaim, though that certainly wasn't reflected at the box office when it was released in 1980. Even the studio had serious doubts about the movie's viability, seeing its strong language, tough characterizations, and stark black-and-white imagery as distinctly uncommercial.

The studio, United Artists, had just had a huge success with *Rocky*, and were looking for a *Rocky II* to follow in its blockbusting footsteps. But *Raging Bull* wasn't that movie. In fact, while paying homage to the style of some of the great fight films of the past, *Raging Bull* isn't a boxing movie as such, despite some of the most graphic scenes of ring violence ever featured in a motion picture.

Extremely violent images (often for their own sake) were nothing new in the cinema of the Seventies, of course, in the work of numerous directors, from Brian De Palma to Michael Winner. But in *Raging Bull*, the candid portrayal of the naked violence that ruled much of La Motta's life via the fight game is just one element that is used to explore the complex emotional battles of its central character—and therein lies its strength.

It was the potential for such a treatment of the Jake La Motta story that attracted Robert De Niro from the start, when he first came across the ex-champ's book. From that time on he wanted to make a movie of *Raging Bull*—and for a long time it was he alone who saw in it a man worth making a film about.

With a dogged determination the actor began lobbying those around him—including producer Irwin Winkler, various studio executives, and his friend and regular collaborator, the director Martin Scorsese. But almost everyone he showed the book to instantly felt that La Motta was simply too "unlikeable" a character to be the subject of any kind of sympathetic treatment—including Scorsese, who had a life-long aversion to boxing in the first place.

But De Niro persisted in his mission of persuasion, seeking out Jake La Motta and his friend (and co-author of the autobiography) Peter Savage in the course of his preliminary research. Eventually, Scorsese, before totally committing himself to the movie, embarked on developing a screenplay with De Niro and scriptwriter Mardik Martin, and later Paul Schrader. After various rewrites that took place against a backdrop of growing personal problems, the director finally said "yes" to De Niro's long-burning ambition.

In retrospect, when De Niro finally convinced him they should make the film, Martin Scorsese's career was at a crossroads. At the time, however, it looked to many that it might be at an end. And even Scorsese himself, when actually making the film, declared more than once that he felt it would be his last.

Via a series of crucial movies, beginning with *Who's That Knocking At My Door?* in 1967, Scorsese had established himself as one of the major names of the new wave of American directors that also included George Lucas, Francis Ford Coppola, Steven Spielberg, and Michael Cimino. But while these contemporaries had made spectacular inroads into the mainstream, with commercial blockbusters from *Star Wars* and *The Godfather* to *ET* and *The Deer Hunter*, at the end of the 1970s Scorsese remained best-recognized for films that were well received and often critically acclaimed, but didn't exactly make box office history. His last major feature before *Raging Bull*, the drama-cum-Hollywood musical *New York, New York*, had been a conspicuous disappointment, and the director was at an all-time low with drug problems which contributed to a critical health crisis.

But once he threw himself into the project after the five years of persuasion by De Niro, he saw it at the time as his final statement on themes he'd been exploring in his most accomplished films so far—namely *Mean Streets* made in 1973, and 1976's *Taxi Driver*. These were issues of identity, self-guilt, and redemption, set against the grim street life of New York City, which drew for their authenticity upon Scorsese's own experience and background.

Scorsese put everything he'd ever learned into the film, with a technical flair that put the black-and-white epic in a league of its own. Every shot was carefully storyboarded, scripted, improvised on set, and scripted again. Every line of dialogue would be played against details (a religious picture here, a background song there) that enhanced its impact. The final picture would be edited, literally at times, inch by inch. The references to filmmaking's past are many; the influences drawn from cinema's history apparent throughout.

But whereas he'd felt during its long and painstaking creation that this would be not just his magnum opus but his swansong as far as feature movies were concerned, it triggered a new creative lease of life for Scorsese. And outside the context of his own highly distinguished career as a filmmaker, it stands as a truly remarkable work on the part of all who contributed to its making—ultimately to be recognized as one of the true monuments of modern cinema.

# architects of a classic

## Scorsese and De Niro

**Martin Scorsese**

Born November 17 1942 in Flushing Long Island, Martin Scorsese grew up in the Sicilian neighborhood of New York City's Little Italy, in Elizabeth Street on the Lower East Side of Manhattan. His parents, Charles and Catherine, were the children of immigrants from Sicily, and had to toil hard just to survive. His father worked in the garment industry, but money was often so short that he'd sometimes earn a little extra lighting gas stoves for Jews on the Sabbath.

As a child, Scorsese's asthmatic condition prevented any strenuous physical exertion, so he spent most of his leisure time in the cinema, sometimes up to three or four times a week—first with his father, then later alone or with teenage friends. He became obsessed with that other world that came alive in the dark of the movie theater, and those early days of picture-going had a profound effect on him as he grew up.

Part of the magic of the cinema, of course, was that you could walk away from it; however involving a particular motion picture might be, you would emerge, eyes blinking to adjust, ears still resounding with the closing music, into the real world. But that solid demarcation between the world of the movies and everyday life certainly didn't apply to the other major influence in the young Scorsese's life—the Catholic Church.

Fascinated by the theatricality and spectacle of its rituals, Scorsese would later compare their impact to that of the great Hollywood biblical epics like *The Robe* and *The Ten Commandments*. Indeed, he would describe years later how his only escape from the grim realities of daily life was in "a movie theater or a church." But, unlike the cinema, the church pervaded every aspect of life, in a society of second-generation immigrants who were only partially integrated into mainstream American society. For Scorsese and those like him, there were few career options outside that of following in his father's footsteps as a menial laborer. And the most prominent of those options were the church or organized crime, both of which had their own codes of honor and "standing" in the community.

Coming from a family with a strong work ethic and church-going commitment, rather than falling into street crime like many of his contemporaries, Scorsese soon found himself part of the church ceremonials as an alter boy at Old St. Patrick's Cathedral (where his parents had married in the 1930s). But the mob and its influence was all around as he grew up, as pervasive a part of the social fabric as the unchallenged authority of the local priest.

There was a third perceived escape route, which the sickly young Scorsese would never have contemplated, and that was sport—where young males from the poorest communities were attracted by the promise of financial gain and social status. This was particularly true of boxing, though for every professional fighter that ever "made it" there were a hundred punch drunk has-beens hanging around East Side bars.

For the adolescent Martin Scorsese, however, the two things that engaged him were his increasing interest in the church, and a consuming passion for the movies. In the first instance, the church attracted his devotion as he began studying for the priesthood, entering a Catholic seminary in 1956 while still in his early teens.

The movies would win in the end, however, when he enrolled at New York University in the early Sixties and began studying filmmaking under Haig Manoogian, whom he would always name as his principal mentor. Significantly, at the end of *Raging Bull*, Scorsese dedicates the film to Manoogian, who died just before its completion.

When he embarked on *Raging Bull*, based on the autobiography of boxer Jake La Motta, it was not the first time that Martin Scorsese had ventured into the New York life of his own upbringing.

The movie, released in 1980, has often been regarded as the second in his "Italian-American" trilogy, between *Mean Streets* in 1973 and 1990's *Goodfellas*. Like those other two works, *Raging Bull*—although ostensibly about boxing— takes a naturalistic look at elements of the second-generation sub-culture of that particular group. The streetwise but otherwise socially inarticulate swaggering of the participants, their overtly coarse and even blasphemous language, the casual reliance on violence as a means to an end—this is the world of Johnny in *Mean Streets*, *Goodfellas*' Jimmy Conway, and Jake La Motta, all played by Robert De Niro. The main difference in Jake's case is that the violence is legitimized when it takes place in the boxing arena— though, as in the other two films, it is endemic to a whole way of life.

## Before Mean Streets

Martin Scorsese had used his native city as a backdrop to other films, right from the beginning of his career after he graduated from the film school of New York University in the mid-1960s. His first full-length feature, *Who's That Knocking At My Door?* in 1967, featured a then-unknown Harvey Keitel as JR, a typical Italian-American on the tough streets of Manhattan. Addressing the issue of Catholic guilt, the story concerns JR's relationship with a local girl, who he intends to marry until he finds out that she was once raped.

Keitel, a fellow student at NYU, appeared in the next Scorsese project, a feature-length documentary called *Street Scenes*. Having worked in various film jobs after *Who's That Knocking*, including the *Woodstock* documentary as assistant director and co-editor, Scorsese embarked—along with students from NYU—on shooting 16mm film at two 1970 anti-Vietnam War demonstrations, in New York and Washington. Cameraman Edward Summer then shot an extended final scene in a Washington hotel room in which Scorsese, Keitel, and others discuss with a large group of students whether the efforts of the protest will result in change or be in vain.

Cult director and producer Roger Corman was responsible for the young filmmaker's first foray west, directing a sequel to his 1970 success *Bloody Mama*. Corman gave Scorsese a budget of just $600,000 and a twenty-four-day schedule to shoot *Boxcar Bertha* (1972) on location in Arkansas, a Depression-set "rural gangster" film along the lines of 1967's highly successful *Bonnie And Clyde*. Corman's B-movie instincts ruled that there had to be some sort of sex or nudity every fifteen minutes, and even insisted on a car chase where one had not been planned, but other than that he basically gave Scorsese a free hand to do as he pleased.

The fact that the young Scorsese turned what was a routine pot-boiler into a decent though not remarkable film says much about his emerging talent, encouraged by the creative freedom afforded him by Corman. The experience with Corman—who had also helped directors like Francis Ford Coppola, James Cameron, and John Sayles—was invaluable. Although the film's characters (even the itinerant hobo Bertha of the title played by Barbara Hershey) never get the chance to develop fully in the face of all the sex and violence, it taught Scorsese valuable lessons in how to make films quickly and cheaply. These were lessons that would impact directly on his first major work, a ground-breaking film that featured Harvey Keitel and Robert De Niro. When Scorsese met the latter through another emergent "movie-brat" director, Brian De Palma, he recognized the young actor from a dozen or more years earlier when they were both teenagers hanging out in adjoining neighborhoods in New York's Little Italy. The movie, set among the "wise-guy" street culture of that same Lower East Side, and released in 1973, was *Mean Streets*.

## Mean Streets

When Scorsese had finished shooting *Boxcar Bertha* he had shown a rough cut to the actor and experimental director John Cassavetes, who bluntly told him he should be doing better things with his talents. Scorsese mentioned he had a script he was developing but which needed rewrites—the older man's advice was to get it done. That script in progress, initially called *Season of the Witch*, would (with the help of scriptwriter Mardik Martin) become *Mean Streets*.

What distinguished *Mean Streets* from Scorsese's film for Corman—and linked it stylistically to *Who's That Knocking*—was the emphasis of characterization over plot. *Bertha* could be said to be heavy on plot—albeit a trivial and sensationalist one—and thin on character development. *Mean Streets* turned out to be just the opposite. Indeed, at one stage, when Scorsese was looking for finance for the film, he approached Roger Corman to see if he was interested. True to form, Corman suggested climbing on the "blaxploitation" band-waggon by hiring an all-black cast. Scorsese, realizing the script was about the people therein rather than the action, declined the idea: "The plot didn't really mean anything. It was the characters that mattered, so I stuck to my guns."

In the character of Charlie, Harvey Keitel was given a role which was in many ways a complex extension of JR in *Who's That Knocking*. Charlie vacillates between a desire for upwardly mobile respectability (he's about to take over running a neighborhood restaurant for a small-time mobster uncle) and a loyalty to De Niro's loose cannon Johnny Boy. Things are further complicated by his interest in Johnny Boy's epileptic cousin Teresa (played by Amy Robinson), but it's the trouble-prone De Niro character which ignites a dynamic performance from Keitel, and vice versa.

Much has been made of the influence of Scorsese's Catholic upbringing in his early movies—and in *Mean Streets* in particular. The personal tensions in Charlie's life are dramatic parallels of the twin pressures of sin and redemption—a dynamic the director would address even more specifically in *Taxi Driver* and *Raging Bull*. And both those films would have De Niro as the central protagonist. In the team of De Niro and Scorsese, *Mean Streets* heralded one of the most creative actor/director relationships in modern cinema.

## Alice Doesn't Live Here Anymore

Although it was a hit in New York, *Mean Streets* didn't do well at the box office across America—despite being well received by the critics. Its success in NYC was partly due to its location, and the fact that it was the talk of the New York Film Festival *and* the Directors' Fortnight at the Cannes Film Festival in 1973.

But it gave Martin Scorsese a firmer foothold in Hollywood, and when the actress Ellen Burstyn was looking for someone to direct a new film she was considering, Francis Ford Coppola suggested she watch *Mean Streets*. Burstyn had just hit with *The Exorcist* for Warners (who'd also distributed *Mean Streets*), and the script she was looking at was called *Alice Doesn't Live Here Anymore*.

The storyline concerns a young widow who decides to travel across country with her young son to Monterey in California to resume a former singing career. The starstruck Alice falls into a relationship with a violent character named Ben (played by Harvey Keitel) while working in a piano bar in Phoenix, Arizona. She leaves for Tucson where—having abandoned her ambition and taken a job as a waitress—she encounters Kris Kristofferson's David, a rich farmer who offers her true love and a settled domesticity. She is still drawn to her dream, however, and, rather than her settling in as the farmer's wife, all three— Alice, David, and 11-year-old Tommy—head for Monterey.

In many ways, *Alice* (released in 1974) would be what used to be called a "woman's" film, were it not for the slightly ambiguous close, where David opts for Monterey after Alice has seemingly agreed to stay in Tucson. That was arrived at by Burstyn and Scorsese (on a suggestion by Kristofferson) after the studio had asked for a conventional "happy-ever-after" ending which they had no intention of agreeing to.

For Scorsese, an important element in making *Alice* was the pure experience of shooting a movie in the (geographically) real West—as opposed to the rural Arkansas of *Bertha*. But, as he would later come to recognize, the result was a far-from-real romantic version of the West which owed much to his life-long obsession with cowboy movies. Having said that, there was an honest realism in the script itself, not least because Scorsese allowed for an element of improvisation on the part of the actors. Again, plot and situation were used to develop and serve characterization rather than the other way round. In the event, the film was a critical and box office success, Ellen Burstyn winning the Oscar for Best Actress. Reviewing the film, critic Richard Combs referred to the director's "particular brand of baroque realism"—a description that could be applied to many of his subsequent works.

This "baroque" element, the attention to often exotic detail, was evidenced in Scorsese's frequent visual references to moments in cinema's past. For the opening sequence of *Alice,* for instance, he cited the unlikely combination of *Duel in the Sun, Gone with the Wind, The Wizard of Oz,* and William Cameron Menzie's cult 1953 sci-fi movie *Invaders from Mars* as inspiration.

## Italianamerican

Once *Alice* was completed, Scorsese returned to New York City where he embarked on a modest-sounding project which nevertheless was to prove to be a pivotal moment in his career.

He'd been approached by the National Endowment for the Humanities to contribute to a series of short television documentaries about America's various immigrant communities, *Storm of Strangers*. Initially he declined the project, assuming what was wanted was a stock historical account with the usual vintage footage and so on. But when he was given the go-ahead to pursue his particular angle on the idea, he produced forty-five minutes of film magic.

His concept was to let two people who had lived first-hand the Italian immigration experience—his mother and father—talk about their coming to America and how their lives developed as a result. Shot over two days around his parents' dinner table, the result was a trigger for crucial elements that emerged in Scorsese's movie-making. With much of it shot on handheld camera, intercut with archive footage and family photographs, the plotless dialogue between the two (some in response to questions compiled by Scorsese's friends) allowed him to explore pure feelings and emotions without the constraints of a "story" to adhere to.

Titled *Italianamerican*, the film was seminal to Scorsese both emotionally and technically. The free flow of conversation from Catherine and Charles Scorsese revealed aspects about them he was never aware of previously. And the nature of the shooting and editing that was necessary taught him an economy of style which he employed in his next full-length project, *Taxi Driver*. It was a pared-down, streamlined approach which would be even more focused in 1980's *Raging Bull*. Of *Italianamerican*, Scorsese simply said it was the best movie he ever made.

## Taxi Driver

The mean streets of New York City were never meaner—or certainly never sleazier—than those cruised by Robert De Niro's Travis Bickle in *Taxi Driver*. But there the similarity with the world of *Mean Streets* ends. Whereas the characters on Scorsese's Italian-American native turf are bound as a community by ties of family, church, and ethnicity, the world of *Taxi Driver* is that of the loner.

Martin Scorsese was offered the script by writer Paul Schrader via Brian De Palma, who had introduced the two in 1972 (and who had introduced the director to De Niro around the same time). It had already by that time done the rounds, but when Scorsese read it he knew that it had to be his next film. Although it had briefly been considered by director Robert Mulligan as a vehicle for Jeff Bridges, the script was now in the hands of producers Julia and Michael Phillips, and when Scorsese expressed an interest in it they agreed to him doing it, as long as De Niro could play anti-hero Travis. After some negotiations with Warner Brothers, who eventually pulled out, Scorsese was finally able to start production on a modest $1.3 million budget in a deal with Columbia.

As with all of Scorsese's character-driven films, casting was crucial. From the first conversation about the part it was obvious that De Niro—who was already familiar with the script—was a perfect choice for the vigilante Vietnam veteran, but the other roles were potentially trickier, particularly that of the thirteen-year-old prostitute Iris. Scorsese was eager to get Jodie Foster, also thirteen at the time, who had appeared in *Alice Doesn't Live Here Anymore*, but there was concern over the nature of the part. Eventually Foster got the job, with her twenty-year-old sister doubling for the most explicit scenes. The part of Betsy, a political campaigner who Travis dates then is rejected by, went to Cybil Shepherd, and long-time Scorsese collaborator Harvey Keitel was chillingly natural as Iris's street-wise pimp.

As with Harvey Keitel's Charlie in *Mean Streets*, Travis's avenging angel personifies the struggle between guilt and redemption. His self-loathing comes from choosing to operate his cab around the city's vilest streets, a "patch" he even indulges in as we see him spending his free hours in porno cinemas. Redemption comes in his attempt to "wash away" what he sees as the "open sewer" of New York; first by a foiled assassination of the politician Betsy campaigns for, then by the successful rescuing of Iris in a cathartic bloodbath. It's an inner conflict that Scorsese would address yet again in the *Raging Bull* persona of Jake La Motta. There the central character acts out his anger, attempting to cast out his demons, in the social context of the Little Italy community and the boxing game. Inside, he's as lonely as Travis Bickle, his self-hatred more ingrained as his career spirals downwards, with no way out. Despite its amoral manifestation, Travis's violence is "virtuous" both in intent and consequence—and he's eventually hailed as a hero by the media. Jake La Motta's brute force, on the other hand, is ultimately self-destructive.

Many of the cinematic devices employed in *Taxi Driver* would be repeated in *Raging Bull*, including the constant view from the main protagonist. We have Travis's observations of street life: his view through the driver mirror of both himself and those he is talking to. We also see through Jake La Motta's eyes—in much of the fight sequences the camera is his eyes as an opponent rains punches to his face. Likewise, different camera speeds are adopted for dramatic effect in both films. Again in *Raging Bull*'s boxing scenes, the seemingly realistic, newsreel-like images are actually presented in disjointed, slowed-down/speeded-up collages, echoing the final slaughter in *Taxi Driver*.

Released in early 1976, *Taxi Driver* was acclaimed as Scorsese's masterpiece. At the time that seemed beyond dispute, but four years later *Raging Bull* would seriously challenge that assertion.

**New York, New York**
Around the time of *Taxi Driver*'s release, Scorsese had embarked on *New York, New York*, set in the big band world of the 1940s and a spectacular homage to one of his great loves, the classic Hollywood musical.

Scorsese was riding on a high by this time. As well as being well received by the critics and at the box office, *Taxi Driver* had won the Palme d'Or, the top prize at the Cannes Film Festival. Ellen Burstyn, meanwhile, had won an Oscar for *Alice Doesn't Live Here Anymore*, as had Robert De Niro (who was starring in *New York, New York*) for his part in *The Godfather Part II*. As shooting started on *New York, New York*, the team, in Scorsese's words, "Started getting cocky. So throw away the script! We improvized a lot and shot a lot of film." That was something of an understatement. As the original budget rose from $7 million to $9 million and an eleven-week shoot grew to twenty, it was clear that self-indulgence had taken over the production. One single song, "Happy Endings," had taken ten days to shoot and cost a third of a million dollars. Even after the twelve-minute film-within-a-film "Happy Endings" —inspired by vintage MGM musicals and Scorsese's favorite part of the movie—was cut, the film was still running to an incredible four-and-a-half hours. Eventually it was cut to just over two-and-a-half, and even shorter in Europe, although a 1981 re-release included "Happy Endings" and ran to about two-and-three-quarter hours.

Despite the film eliciting strong performances from De Niro as jazz saxophonist Jimmy Doyle and Liza Minnelli as his band vocalist girlfriend Francine, critics—and in retrospect Scorsese—felt it fell between two stools. On the one hand, the director played to his stated intention of a celebration of the great movie musicals with lots of color, extravagant sets, and inspiring, uplifting songs. On the other hand, he couldn't get away from his personal instinct to put character before plot and situation. What we have, therefore, is the friction between angst-ridden Jimmy's jealousy and Francine's success, grittily played by De Niro and Minnelli in often improvised sequences, spelled out in the inappropriately spectacular visual context of a 1950s musical.

And spectacular the movie certainly was, with evocative sets by production designer Boris Leven, whose films included *Giant* (1956), *West Side Story* (1961), and *The Sound of Music* (1965), and the sort of soaring camerawork and overhead shots associated with the seminal musicals of Vincente Minnelli—Liza's father. Viewed in retrospect, *New York, New York* is an immensely enjoyable, exhilarating film, despite the seeming incompatibility of Scorsese's parallel ambitions for it. But before he plunged himself back into the far-from-glamorous and (literally) less colorful world of the "real" 1940s Manhattan of *Raging Bull*, Martin Scorsese would indulge his love of music *per se* in a feature-length documentary, *The Last Waltz*.

## The Last Waltz

The shooting of *New York, New York*—fraught in itself, given the largely self-inflicted problems of schedule and budget—coincided with an equally difficult period in Scorsese's personal life. His marriage to his second wife Julia Cameron, who was expecting their child at the time, was not going well. In her subsequent divorce action, Cameron cited both Scorsese's increasing drug use and an alleged affair with Liza Minnelli. The latter was never substantiated, but his drug use (which, it was rumored, was rife on the set of *New York, New York*) was symptomatic of a dark period in his life which would eventually resolve itself with the making of *Raging Bull*.

During this period his friend (and mutual drug-buddy at the time) Robbie Robertson, guitarist with The Band, approached Scorsese about filming the group's final concert, to take place at the end of November 1976—a month after the filming of *New York, New York* was due to wind up. (The director had already worked on musical documentaries in an editorial capacity—on *Woodstock* in 1970, *Medicine Ball Caravan* (1971), and *Elvis On Tour* in 1972.) After sixteen years on the road, The

Band had decided to play their final gig on Thanksgiving Day at the Winterland Ballroom in San Francisco.

With the main performance footage shot in one night through the seven-hour concert, the film was intercut with interviews conducted with The Band in their recording studio, and three songs performed and filmed on the MGM soundstage. The end result was an evocation of not just the music of The Band and the stellar list of guests that night (including Muddy Waters, Dr. John, Eric Clapton, Emmylou Harris, Joni Mitchell, Bob Dylan, and many more), but of the rock and roll life which Robertson and his fellow musicians (as a group at least) were stepping out of. The camera swoops and glides over the stage with the music—for Scorsese, after *New York, New York*, it was undoubtedly a liberating experience. With other projects on the go through 1977, *The Last Waltz* wasn't released until 1978.

In the meantime, Martin Scorsese's own physical health was deteriorating—his version of the rock and roll lifestyle was taking its toll. In the late summer of 1978 he was hospitalized with internal bleeding, and realized things had to change: "I guess I did it all, so it was now time to move on."

It was while Scorsese was in hospital that Robert De Niro visited him and finally convinced him that he should make *Raging Bull*, from the Jake La Motta autobiography he had given him a couple of years earlier. "I understood then what Jake was, but only having gone through a similar experience" Scorsese would recall, "The decision to make the film was made then". He was about to embark on what many still consider his greatest film, and cast out his own demons in the process.

## Robert De Niro

Born on August 17 1943 in New York City, Robert De Niro grew up in the cosmopolitan environment of Greenwich Village. His parents were both artists. His father, also Robert, was a painter, sculptor, and poet, his mother Virginia a painter who also supplemented her income writing stories for pulp crime magazines.

Following his first stage role, at the age of ten, playing the cowardly lion in the *Wizard of Oz*, the young Bobby didn't hit the stage again for seven years. In his early teens he was attracted by the gangs of Italian kids starting to appear on the east end of Bleecker Street where he lived, and he fell in with one such group of street-wise youngsters—his pallid looks earning him the nickname "Bobby Milk". Despite his initially solitary nature, he soon adopted the gang's leather jacket style and confident swagger. This might have been small-time gang stuff, but it was for real.

School-wise he was very much the archetypal drop-out, and after a trip hitch-hiking around Europe when he was sixteen, he announced to a somewhat surprised mother (his parents had separated some time earlier) that he was going to train to be an actor. His inspiration was the only acting he'd ever regularly witnessed, as with most kids of his generation, up on the cinema screen.

De Niro studied with the top two drama coaches in New York—Stella Adler at her Conservatory of Acting, and Lee Strasberg in the Actor's Studio, both proponents of rival versions of the Method style of acting. His first paying role came when he was still seventeen, in a touring performance of Chekhov's *The Bear*, after which a decade of off-Broadway and dinner theater roles would follow during which he made just minor inroads into movies.

## The big screen beckons

His very first appearance on film was a supporting part in a film directed by the then little-known Brian De Palma, *The Wedding Party*. Shot in 1963, the slight comedy featured De Niro (playing a character called Robert De Nero!) as one of two friends who first try to prevent another friend's marriage, only to later chase him down to force him into it. It wasn't released until 1969, when it went largely unnoticed.

Next came an uncredited walk-on part as a customer in a diner, in a French film *Trois Chambres à Manhattan* (*Three Rooms in Manhattan*) directed in 1965 by Marcel Carné. Following that, three years passed before De Niro was in his next movie, another De Palma picture, *Greetings!* (1968). In a quirky satire on free-love, the Vietnam War, and the Sixties counterculture, he played would-be filmmaker and "Peeping Tom" Jon Rubin, receiving some good notices for the comedy role. But, although he'd yet to get real attention for his screen work, De Niro's movie parts were now becoming more regular.

1969 saw one of the most bizarre projects in his film career, when he was cast as a movie-maker yet again. Featuring a vacuous plot, *Sam's Song* concerned a New York film man, Sam, at a party thrown by some wealthy Long Islanders. De Niro equipped himself perfectly well in the title role, but the film (an experimental "arthouse" exercise on the part of director Jordan Leondopolous) was never intended for a proper release at the time. More irritating to De Niro than the lack of exposure the film afforded him, was when it appeared years later under another title in a radically altered form (and, crucially, between two of the most important releases of his career: 1978's *The Deer Hunter* and *Raging Bull* in 1980). The powerful Cannon group had acquired the rights to the *Sam's Song* footage, and got director John Broderick to shoot an extra plotline with new actors, starting with Sam's murder. Re-titled *The Swap* (and also known as *Line of Fire*), the 1979 release was a blatant cash-in on De Niro's status as one of the biggest names in Hollywood.

## On the way up

After *Sam's Song* came *Bloody Mama* and, although not exactly a milestone in De Niro's Hollywood career, it marked the first discernable instance of a personal approach to characterization on his part. The 1970 film, by cult exploitation director Roger Corman, was (like its Scorsese-directed 1972 sequel *Boxcar Bertha*) a typically Corman-esque take on the 1967 success of Arthur Penn's *Bonnie and Clyde*.

De Niro got the part via the Hollywood veteran Shelley Winters, who—while still acting—had taken on a tutorial role at Lee Strasberg's Actor's Studio. The actress saw potential in the young De Niro from the start, and when she accepted the lead in *Bloody Mama* as the real-life 1920s outlaw Kate Barker, she recommended her protégé for the portrayal of one of her sons, dope-addicted Lloyd.

True to his Method training, De Niro immersed himself in the character during the Arkansas-based location work, to the point where he would remain seemingly half-stoned hours after a shoot. He even went so far as to eavesdrop on the conversations of local folk, so he could perfect their speech rhythms. And, taking his Method training one bit further, he was able to "construct" the character of Lloyd element by element, right down to his turn of phrase or way of walking. It was the first real sign of a discipline he'd bring to bear in all his work, creating unforgettable characters, be they fictional like Travis Bickle or based on real life, as with Jake La Motta.

The same year that *Bloody Mama* was released, 1970, also saw another project with Brian De Palma, *Hi, Mom!* A straightforward sequel to *Greetings*, De Niro reprized his role as Jon Rubin, still the "Peeping Tom", but now returning from Vietnam. This time, however, the character was far more developed, more substantial—and, as Jon blows up the building where he lives with his demanding wife, then berates a TV crew about the dangers of New York before greeting his mother ("Hi, Mom!") via the live cameras, more like a scary premonition of Travis in *Taxi Driver*.

Robert De Niro's next three films were all released in 1971, and all flops, either with the critics or at the box office, or both. The first two, *Jennifer On My Mind* and *Born To Win*, were both set in the context of the burgeoning hard drug scene that came in the wake of the counterculture embracing soft drugs in the late Sixties. *Jennifer On My Mind* deals with two of the "beautiful people" who fall foul of heroin while also falling in love, while *Born To Win* (also known as *Born To Lose* and later *The Addict*) followed the downward spiral of J, a once-successful hairdresser who now runs errands for a heroin dealer in order to feed his own $100-a-day habit. In *Jennifer* De Niro appeared way down the cast list as an unlicensed "gypsy" cab driver, and had similar billing in *Born To Win* as one of the cops who sets up J and his girlfriend in order to get to the dealer. Both were hardboiled parts that did him no harm as far as screen experience was concerned.

De Niro's third release in 1971, *The Gang That Couldn't Shoot Straight*, had the more promising prospect of being adapted from a novel by humorous writer Jimmy Breslin, loosely based on the real-life Brooklyn mob family of Joey Gallo. The film got off to a bad start—De Niro, who played a kleptomaniac Italian pulling strings to stay in the US, was replacing Al Pacino, who'd dropped out when he was made an offer he couldn't refuse—a part in *The Godfather*. Then Italian star Marcello Mastroianni dropped out of the lead part, the lesser-known Jerry Orbach taking his place. All in all, the movie seemed doomed from the set-off, and this was reflected in the critical panning it received—though for De Niro, who called it "my first big-deal movie," it was another step forward.

But it was in 1973 that heads really began to turn in De Niro's direction, after he passed a rigorous auditioning process for the lead role in *Bang The Drum Slowly*, in which he would play Bruce Pearson, a dying baseball player. Again he brought his Method training into play, mastering details such as the fictional character's habit of chewing tobacco, and spending three weeks in Georgia to pick up the correct accent. So immersed did he become in the character that he apparently admonished a wardrobe mistress when she joked about Pearson being dull-witted. It was Robert De Niro's first lead part in a film, and won him the 1974 New York Film Critics award for Best Actor.

### Johnny Boy to Jake

Late in 1972, Martin Scorsese offered De Niro a part in a movie he had just started shooting in Manhattan's Little Italy,

*Mean Streets*. Even though De Niro wasn't offered the lead—
that had already gone to Harvey Keitel—his stunning
performance in the role of wise-guy Johnny Boy would be
the beginning of a long and fruitful working relationship
between the actor and director. It was a relationship that
would never be bettered than in what many considered to be
both artists' greatest work, eight years and three more
collaborations later, *Raging Bull*.

De Niro would enjoy a more immediate triumph, however,
with the part of Vito Corleone in *Part II* of 1972's hugely
successful *The Godfather*. Director Francis Ford Coppola's new
film wasn't a sequel as such, tracing the history of the
Corleone family from earlier years with De Niro playing the
younger version of Marlon Brando's Don Corleone from the
original movie. Released in 1974, it went on to garner even
more Academy Awards than its Oscar-winning predecessor,
winning in six categories including Best Picture, Script,
Director, and, for Robert De Niro, Best Supporting Actor.
His personal success in the film consolidated for De Niro a
growing reputation as Hollywood's "new" Marlon Brando.

Through 1974 and 1975, De Niro spent a lot of time in
Italy, working with the director Bernardo Bertolucci. The
project was a sprawling epic, following the struggles and
tensions between two men, one born of peasant stock
(played by Gerard Depardieu), the other born to a land owner
(De Niro) as the country was ideologically split between
Communists and Fascists in the first half of the twentieth
century. Titled simply *1900*, the film ran to nearly five-and-a-
half hours and is usually shown in two parts. Widely regarded
as an ill-judged indulgence on the director's part when it first

appeared in 1976, it nevertheless confirmed De Niro's strength in the most demanding of roles.

When he was approached to play in a film directed by Elia Kazan, De Niro was naturally elated. Kazan was the veteran director who was most closely associated with the first Hollywood manifestation of the Method school of acting, and instrumental in the launching of both Marlon Brando and James Dean. The film, released in 1976, was an adaptation by British playwright Harold Pinter of F. Scott Fitzgerald's unfinished novel *The Last Tycoon*, in which De Niro played an old-school movie producer who is literally working himself to death. With a cast that included Robert Mitchum, Tony Curtis, Jeanne Moreau, Jack Nicholson, and Donald Pleasance, the film turned out to be a surprisingly lackluster affair, with De Niro's performance one of its few redeeming factors. But while still shooting the Kazan picture, which some had thought would finally establish his reputation in "mainstream" Hollywood, De Niro had finished making the movie that would actually confirm his undisputed status (and that of Martin Scorsese) once and for all, a film which was the complete antithesis of the star-studded but ultimately lightweight *Last Tycoon*.

In *Taxi Driver*'s Travis Bickle (for which he was nominated for an Oscar), De Niro would seem to have found his perfect niche. The troubled, amoral anti-hero, seeking his own redemption in the violent "cleansing" of society's ills, was an ideally complex character for him to sink himself into. Indeed, so powerful was his performance that it seemed to become an instant De Niro "stereotype" (as Stanley Kowalski in 1951's *A Streetcar Named Desire* became for Brando), even though the actor never replicated it in any subsequent role.

As if to prove the point, his next outing with Scorsese (released a year later, in 1977) would be a total departure from *Taxi Driver* both in subject matter and context, despite its title *New York, New York*. The part of 1940s saxophone player Jimmy Doyle was just as complex, however. De Niro threw himself into the role wholeheartedly, as was now his norm, even learning the rudiments of playing the instrument in the process. However, in making a film which called for intense characterization but at the same time was a spectacular *homage* to the classic Hollywood musical, Scorsese may have overreached himself. And it would be three years before the actor and director's next collaboration, *Raging Bull,* hit the screen—stylistically as much a contrast to *New York, New York* as the musical had been to *Taxi Driver*.

In the meantime, De Niro appeared in another Oscar-nominated role which immediately took its place among the memorable screen performances of the 1970s. It was the part of Michael, the Vietnam serviceman from a steel town in Pennsylvania, in an epic that was more concerned with the *effect* of war on its participants and their home community than it was with the actual hostilities. Despite being savaged by some "liberal" critics for its apparent sentimental patriotism, Michael Cimino's *The Deer Hunter* (1978) was ultimately an anti-war film, showing the futility of conflict through the lives of ordinary Americans that were forever changed by the experience.

By the time *The Deer Hunter* opened in cinemas at the end of 1978, Robert De Niro had finally convinced an initially doubtful Scorsese that they should make a movie out of Jake La Motta's *Raging Bull* autobiography.

# a raging voice
## From autobiography to screenplay

First published in 1970 by the American publishers Prentice Hall, former middleweight boxing champion Jake La Motta's autobiography *Raging Bull: My Story* was written in a prose that one review called "as straightforward and at times as brutal as his style in the ring."

It was written by La Motta with two co-authors: Joseph Carter, a Harvard-educated journalist whose other books included a work about Italian Renaissance painting and a history of the French constitution, and Peter Savage, a life-long friend and business associate of La Motta who figures in the book as Pete Petrella. Savage would go on to direct and produce low-budget films of his own (in which La Motta appeared), as well as acting in an advisory capacity on the *Raging Bull* movie. Boston-born Joseph Carter died in 1984.

### Bronx bully

Giacobe (Jake) La Motta was born on July 10 1921, the son of an immigrant father from Messina in Sicily and an Italian mother born in New York. His father, Joe La Motta, settled in the northern part of Manhattan's Lower East Side, around 10$^{th}$ Street and First Avenue, just after the end of World War I, and that was where Jake was born and spent his early childhood.

Now trendified as the East Village, back then the district was—like most of the Lower East Side—a slum. By the time

Jake was six or seven, however, the family had moved to what he described as "another great slum," this time in Philadelphia, and it was there that he started to learn the tough lessons of the street. His father, who used to beat Jake frequently, showed him little affection. His mother, who *did* show the child love, was likewise the target of her husband's physical abuse. And it was his father who inculcated to him the notion that the only way to survive was by sheer brute aggression.

In his book Jake tells how, when he was eight or so, he came home from school one day, crying to his mother that some kids had ganged up on him and stolen the sandwich she had made for his lunch. His father turned on him in a fury, slapping him across the face while thrusting an ice pick into his hand, telling the child if he was attacked again to retaliate with the pick. If he came home crying again, his father threatened, there would be a worse beating awaiting him than he'd ever get in the playground. The next time he was set upon the young Jake used the ice pick on his assailants, who fled as he ripped into the cheek of one of them: "I can still remember that feeling of power flood through me." From then on his father's advice of "hit 'em first and hit 'em hard" stayed with him. He soon learned to use his fists, harder and faster than any of the other kids—street fighting became the norm, and he usually came out on top.

Another move took the family—Jake, his parents, brother Joe, and sisters—back to New York City, this time to the Bronx and another slum dwelling. He confesses in the book how the only things he learned when he was at school were the things they didn't teach: fighting and stealing. He was already full of anger at the world around him—his father who beat him, teachers and preachers who tried to put him straight, even kids who he thought were teasing him on account of a hearing disability brought on by the cold in the tenements.

As he grew from a troublesome child to an angry adolescent he tells how his rage manifested itself in more street violence and petty crime. He was the archetypal teenage hooligan, ready to take his anger out on any hapless individual who should invoke his slightest displeasure, while his delinquency extended to shoplifting, mugging, and "knocking off" candy stores. One particularly horrific incident was to haunt him for the rest of his life. He mugged a local bookie who he knew would be carrying a sizeable sum in cash, hitting him over the head with a piece of lead piping. But his victim started to get up so La Motta hit him again, and again—"I lost my head. I wanted to kill him"—until he finally collapsed. The next day he read in the newspapers that the bookie had been found dead in the alley where he had left him. He now had a murder on his conscience.

After an attempted robbery on a jewelry store he served time in the inevitable reform school, the Coxsackie Correctional Institution in upstate New York, and it was there that his violent streak, never far from the surface, was channeled into training as a boxer in the school gymnasium. A fellow inmate was Rocco Barbella, who Jake had run around with on the latter's Lower East Side patch when things were quiet in the Bronx. As Rocky Graziano, Barbella would win the world middleweight title in 1947, two years before La Motta, and go on to write his own autobiography, *Somebody Up There Likes Me*, which became a hit film for Paul Newman in 1956—by which time La Motta had won and lost the title, and seen his career swiftly go down the pan.

**Battling to the top**

As soon as he was released from reform school, Jake decided that boxing was the route to make something of his life, and as an undefeated amateur felled most of his 21 opponents in a knock-out. His trademark bull-like charges and non-stop punching in the ring earned him the nickname "The Bronx Bull," and in 1940 he won the New York State Diamond Belt as a light-heavyweight.

He had his first professional fight in 1941, winning a four-round decision over Charley Mackley. A spectacular string of victories over the next two years culminated in a ten-round win over the great Sugar Ray Robinson in February, 1943. It was Robinson's first loss as a professional, and his only defeat in 218 bouts stretching from the late 1930s to the early 1950s. But through this seemingly unstoppable rise to the top of the fight game, Jake La Motta still couldn't keep his anger—and out-of-the-ring violence—in check. Those closest to him were often the immediate targets—girlfriends, wives, colleagues, and also the Mob, who continually frustrated his ambition of going for the title because he refused to throw a fight.

The text of La Motta's book, which Scorsese felt was largely the work of Jake's collaborator Peter Savage—"Pete explaining Jake to Jake"—reverberates with that anger. It was a fury that wasn't assuaged after he relented and turned to the Mob for a short-cut to the world middleweight belt, which he won in 1949 against the Frenchman Marcel Cerdan. Altogether through 106 fights he pummeled his way to no less than 83 victories, holding the championship title for two years.

La Motta defended his title twice, eventually losing it to his old rival Sugar Ray Robinson who knocked him out in the 13th round in a sensational bout in February 1951. In a bloody finish, a badly battered La Motta avoided being knocked down by hanging onto the ropes while he was counted out. From then on, the "Bronx Bull" was still a raging bull, but now on a self-inflicted downward spiral.

Fed by the guilt of the bookie murder he thought he'd committed as a teenager, when he discovered his victim was actually alive and well (the newspaper that reported the crime had simply got it wrong), the spark of guilt that had ignited his passion was extinguished. By 1953 he'd retired from the fight game, a defeated and broken ex-champ. From there it wasn't far—via crumbling finances, a divorce, drink and drug problems, and a child prostitution charge—to a six-month stretch in prison.

**After the fall**
After prison, where he finally found redemption for his guilt, Jake sought vindication. By the 1960s, he was a bloated caricature of his former self, introducing the girls at a strip club and doing the stand-up nightclub act that opens and concludes the movie.

Subsequent to the period covered in Scorsese's film, the book goes on to describe how, at the end of the 1970s, La Motta was playing bit parts on the stage, television, and in exploitation movies. He even appeared in a major film (though not mentioned in his book) as a bartender in the 1961 Paul Newman poolroom classic *The Hustler*. And via his book he became a whistle-blower on the corruption within the boxing business, telling of the set-ups he had to be part of in order to become champ.

Jake La Motta's late-in-the-day involvement in movies and television came partly through film contacts picking up on his nightclub act, and by way of his old crony Pete Savage (whose character was combined with Jake's brother Joey in the *Raging Bull* film) who, unlikely though it seems, had started making films himself by the early 1970s.

It was perhaps surprising, therefore, that no-one had developed *Raging Bull* into a screenplay by the time Robert De Niro came across the book—and it would be another seven years before a movie version finally hit the big screen.

## An idea takes shape

It was in Italy in late 1973, when De Niro was about to start filming *1900* with Bernardo Bertolucci, that the actor first read Jake La Motta's autobiography. The book immediately made a strong impression on him, as he would tell the *New York Times* in 1980: "There was something about it—a strong thrust, a portrait of a direct man without complications. Something at the center of it was very good for me. I felt I could evolve into the character."

From the start, De Niro could see the cinematic possibilities in the book, not just in the character but also in the subject matter. Jake's narrative (or as Scorsese would later point out, Pete Savage's interpretation of Jake's narrative) was peppered with allusions to images from the cinema. Early on in the book he conjures up an image of his memories as a *film noir*, comparing his recollections of the past to "looking at an old black-and-white movie … with no musical score, just sometimes the sound of a police siren or pistol shot … and almost all of it happens at night, as if I lived my whole life at night."

Hoping Scorsese would be similarly enthusiastic about the book, De Niro gave it to him when the director was working on *Alice Doesn't Live Here Anymore*. "I called Marty about it and said 'You know this book is not so well written, but it's got some heart to it, there's something interesting about the story' so then he got a copy and read it." Even that early on, according to Scorsese, De Niro talked about playing the character of La Motta and even had in mind the necessary physical transformation he would have to make to play the part.

But at first Scorsese wasn't convinced—a reaction not helped by the fact that he simply didn't like boxing. He would later admit that, at the time, the only "logical" boxing scene he ever saw in a movie was in a Buster Keaton silent comedy, where Keaton, as his opponent in the ring lunges towards him, hits the guy with one of the corner stools!

But De Niro was persuasive, and Scorsese came to recognize that there were interesting elements to the book that *could* perhaps be developed into a film. "So from that point on he kept checking in with me, and I kept going off in different directions, and one of them was *Taxi Driver*, and then we did *New York, New York* together, and he was still being serious about *Raging Bull*," Scorsese would recall.

Over the next few years, while they were planning and making *Taxi Driver* and *New York, New York*, the two men threw ideas around about adapting *Raging Bull* for the screen. Scorsese went so far as to contact La Motta's friend and co-writer Pete Savage, who even ended up with bit parts in both *Taxi Driver* and *New York, New York*.

Nothing concrete happened, however. There was talk at one point of producing a stage version entitled *Prize Fighter*, performing it live at night while filming it in the daytime. That came to nothing, as did a script developed by Scorsese's *Mean Streets* and *New York, New York* collaborator, Mardik Martin, who had also been party to the stage play idea— "Bob [De Niro] decided that he wanted to try some of his dialogue in a play. So I actually sat down and I wrote the first act … I'd never written a play before, but I thought 'what's the big deal?' "

When they gave him the project, Martin spent six months on the initial research, much of it in the company of De Niro. They sat through what Martin would describe as "every boxing movie ever made," in order to both learn from them and to make sure they didn't repeat any of the clichés. The two flew down to Miami and spent three or four days with Vickie La Motta (Jake's second wife) listening to her retell stories of her time with Jake. Eventually, after nearly two years working on the script through various versions, Martin felt it was time to move on—and the feeling was mutual. Scorsese felt bad about dropping Martin (although he'd still not committed himself to the project at this stage), who he valued as both a writer he could work with and old friend from his days at NYU film school. But he felt he couldn't do anything with the writer's script (in which various characters' versions of the story were developed in parallel). Scorsese compared it to *Rashomon*, the 1951 film by Japanese director Akira Kurosawa that featured four different personal perspectives of the same incident.

It was only when Scorsese was at his lowest ebb, after coughing up blood at the Telluride Film Festival and collapsing with an internal hemorrhage when he returned to New York—"The next thing I knew I was in the emergency ward at the New York Hospital"—that he could begin to see the similarities between his situation and elements of Jake La Motta's story. "I was always angry," he would say of that hedonistic period in his life that had led to this physical crisis, "throwing glasses, provoking people, really unpleasant to be around. I always found, no matter what anybody said, something to take offence at."

"I didn't think I was going to make the film, quite honestly. I was going off in my own direction, and I had my own issues with the work I was doing, and I was going through my own sort of crisis ... so it reached a point where it really came down to De Niro's insistence." So when Robert De Niro raised the subject of *Raging Bull* yet again, at Scorsese's hospital bedside during the 1978 Labor Day weekend, this time he gave it to him straight—either he rose to the challenge or threw in the towel: "Are you going to be one of those flash-in-the-pan directors who does a few good movies and it's over for them?" But now the director knew the time was right to go with it: "I used *Raging Bull* as a kind of rehabilitation."

### The final script

Once Scorsese had given the project a definite green light, he and De Niro met with *Taxi Driver* screenwriter Paul Schrader at the famous Hollywood restaurant Musso and Frank's, and persuaded him to come on board. Taking over from where Mardik Martin had left off, Schrader reshaped the latter's various drafts, revisiting his research material, and gradually coming up with what would be the basic structure of the film.

It was Schrader's idea, for instance, to "bookend" the film with Jake's nightclub routine, opening with his "That's entertainment" speech in the dressing room before cutting to him being punched in the face during his first major defeat in the ring, and closing with him leaving the room to go on stage. Scorsese was particularly excited about this approach, cutting right into the center of the story and beginning it there, rather than going to the "real" beginning with a linear narrative.

Another major change that Schrader made was to include Jake's brother Joey, who hadn't appeared at all in Martin's script. Schrader felt the angle of the sibling who started out as a boxer like Jake but ended up managing his brother was worth exploring. "I discovered that there were in fact two fighting La Motta brothers, they were two fighters together, and they sometimes shared the bill together. Joey had the gift of the gab and was personable, while Jake was socially really quite awkward. So they made a kind of *de facto* deal between themselves ... essentially Joey would manage Jake and get the girls, Jake would get the beatings and then they'd split the money." Schrader also felt that the sibling element allowed them to get back into what he called "classic storytelling, back into *East of Eden* ... all the elements that are involved in a two-brother story."

Other modifications included a less harrowing version of the infamous incident over an overcooked steak, when La Motta beat his pregnant wife up and kicked her in the stomach, causing a miscarriage. In Schrader's version he simply knocks her out, while in the final movie you just see Jake overturning the table, pushing his wife into the bedroom and shutting the door.

There were, in fact, many elements in Schrader's script that Scorsese and De Niro still weren't happy about, so they decided to rework it (with the writer's agreement) into what they hoped would be a near-to-final draft. With that in mind, the two took off to the West Indies island of St. Martin ("... hard for me, because as far as I'm concerned, there's only one island, Manhattan," Scorsese would wryly recall), where for the next two-and-a-half weeks they hammered out their rewrite, scene by scene. It was physically hard for Scorsese, just out of hospital and still in a weak condition, but, as he would later admit, "Bob got me through it"—the actor waking him up in the morning, making coffee, and generally pushing things along. Dialogue was changed, some characters combined— "In fact [we] rewrote the entire picture."

A case in point was the final scene, in which Jake reprises Marlon Brando's back-of-the-taxi speech in *On The Waterfront* (a poignant parallel to La Motta's own "one way ticket to palookaville" downfall) in front of the dressing room mirror. Schrader originally planned to also feature him quoting Shakespeare, Tennessee Williams et al, before Scorsese and De Niro decided to keep it to the utterly apt *Waterfront* piece. They had discussed the matter some time earlier with Scorsese's friend, the great British director Michael Powell, who thought the "Shakespeare" ending was all wrong. It was then that they decided to seriously consider just the speech from *On The Waterfront*, as Scorsese would recall: "We were discussing it, and it came up that it was more *our* iconography than, for better or worse ... Shakespeare, or Christopher Marlowe, or Ben Jonson ... the fact is it was more our iconography being American, with our education, with our background, this is where we come from. So we surrendered to it, and said 'OK, let's do it.' "

They also wrote out the most explicitly sexual scenes, including one in a Florida jail cell where Jake pounds his fist against the wall after being unable to masturbate. De Niro replaced it with the boxer beating his head as well as his fists on the stone, shouting "Why, why, why?" Although Schrader felt his three-minute monologue would have been welcomed by De Niro—"an actor's treat"—De Niro simply felt it didn't fit the character of Jake La Motta. "I don't know where Paul got that, but that had nothing to do with anything I remember about Jake, or what Marty and I felt about what we were trying to do."

Similarly, although we see Jake shoving ice down his shorts to douse an erection during pre-fight celibacy, we don't actually see his penis. "De Niro was baulking at a lot of the heavier stuff" Schrader would recall in Peter Biskind's book *Easy Riders, Raging Bulls*." 'Why do we have to do these things?' Marty wasn't going to take on Bob, because he had to work with him, so he was letting me fight those fights. It was a bold, original kind of scene. But looking at it from De Niro's point of view, it was pretty hard to make it work, sitting there with your dick in your hand."

The rewrite also dispensed with Jake's friend Pete Petrella (Peter Savage), the character being merged into that of brother Joey as the close ally who La Motta would accuse of sleeping with his wife, and go on to savagely attack in front of his family. "It was dramatically efficient to combine the two characters into one and make it the brother, make it bound by blood," Scorsese explained when looking back on the film twenty-five years later.

When they showed their revised script to Paul Schrader, the screenwriter wasn't exactly keen on many of the changes to his work, but went along with it. And when shooting began on the movie, he sent them a telegram in which he wrote "Jake did it his way, I did it my way, you do it your way" just to ensure the director wouldn't feel he was upsetting him by altering the script. But there was no way Scorsese was going to downgrade Schrader's (or indeed Martin's) contribution to the screenplay, the two being given full on-screen credit without a mention of his or De Niro's part in the process.

Just as the final *Waterfront* monologue had, in Scorsese's own words, "De Niro playing Jake La Motta playing Marlon Brando playing Terry Malone," so the entire script was the result of a similar layering process. It started with La Motta's own reminiscences, was filtered and (no doubt) embellished textually by Joseph Carter and Peter Savage, before ending up as a finished book. That was then used as a starting point by Mardik Martin, from which Schrader developed a full-blown screenplay, which in turn was chopped, changed, and edited by De Niro and Scorsese.

What ended up as a "final" version, subject to more modifications on set, would be the basis for one of the greatest boxing movies—though in many respects an anti-boxing movie—ever to come out of Hollywood. But they had to sell the idea to the studios first.

Producers Irwin Winkler and Robert Chartoff, having financed *New York, New York*, were keen on the project, especially when they read De Niro and Scorsese's final draft. They knew the subject well, Robert Chartoff recalling how, when he was a kid from the Bronx, everyone regarded Jake

La Motta as "one of our own" who they all identified with. Winkler tells how De Niro first raised the subject of a film, when every day on the set of *New York, New York* he'd be walking round with a "shop-worn-looking book—he never told me what it was but he always carried it around." Until one day the actor said he'd like Winkler to take a look at it. It was, of course, the La Motta autobiography.

United Artists, who had likewise been responsible for *New York, New York*, weren't so easily convinced. What they really wanted was another *Rocky*. Released in 1976, *Rocky*, starring Sylvester Stallone, was the most successful boxing movie of recent years, and had won an Academy Award for Best Picture in the process. The studio and Chartoff/Winkler jointly owned the copyright on the film, and when the two producers approached them about another fight film, UA naturally began thinking along the lines of the previous blockbuster.

The first problem with *Raging Bull* as far as the studio was concerned was that Scorsese intended to film it in black and white—especially after *Rocky* and other boxing films of the Seventies had all been shot in color. And, despite De Niro's "toning down" of some of the sex from Schrader's draft, they still felt nervous about the script's excessive use of "bad" language. At that time, however, directors like Scorsese had a lot of power, especially when they were in a winning combination as he was perceived to be with De Niro. He soon convinced UA that this was a serious film for adults which nevertheless could do well at the box office, and as far as shooting in monochrome was concerned, he argued that it served to distance the movie from other contemporary boxing epics.

The studio agreed to do the picture and, six years after he'd first been captivated by Jake La Motta's autobiography, Robert De Niro was at last about to recreate the character on the cinema screen.

# hollywood in the ring

## Boxing movies and film noir

Despite Martin Scorsese's apparent dismissal of the boxing movie as such when he cited Buster Keaton's *Battling Butler* (1926) as the only film that had the right attitude to the sport, there was a strong tradition in Hollywood of fight films that de-glamorized boxing as effectively as Keaton and in a far more graphic and hard-hitting way.

### The big fight

The traditional fight movie had its heyday in the late Forties and early Fifties in a handful of *film noir* classics that used the sport, its essential violence and inevitable corruption, as a metaphor for inner conflicts within its participants and the moral bankruptcy of the world it occupied.

While preparing for *Raging Bull*, Scorsese showed De Niro a 16mm print of *Body and Soul*, directed by Robert Rossen in 1947 with John Garfield as the up-and-coming boxer up against tough choices in the face of fight-game corruption. Scorsese would recall seeing boxing matches in cinemas when he was a kid, remembering they didn't hold his attention too long as they always seemed to be shot from the same angle. Once he started researching *Raging Bull, Body and Soul* was one of the films that revealed the possibilities of a genre he'd previously had no ambitions to emulate. In it the master camerman James Wong Howe got *into* the ring, literally *with* the fighters, moving around them on roller skates for some of the hand-held action shots.

Nominated for three Oscars, *Body and Soul* was followed in 1949 by two more classics of the genre. *Champion*, which received six nominations, featured Kirk Douglas in one of his strongest roles as "Midge" Kelly, a champ who is increasingly seduced by his fame and fortune. Corrupted by his success, self-loathing sets in as he concedes to one thrown fight after another. Finally he fights to win, like a wild man battling against not just his opponent in the ring but those who would control his destiny inside and outside it. He wins with a knock-out, but then dies from brain damage.

There are many parallels in the *Champion* storyline with Jake La Motta's story. Initially presented with some sympathy, the screenplay's sub-plot traces the boxer's persecution complex, from a poverty-stricken background to his full-scale paranoia and alienation.

The same year, Robert Ryan appeared in Robert Wise's *The Set-Up* as Stoker Thompson, a fighter who like Douglas's *Champion* is a pawn in the hands of the fight-game racketeers. In the movie's climactic end match, the now-broken hero is so past his best that his managers assume he'll lose anyway—they don't even bother to tell him it's another fight he has to throw. But, in a sudden burst of indignant anger and belated self-respect, he asserts his old form and wins the contest—only to be pursued and badly beaten up by the fixers' thugs immediately afterwards. The ring becomes a symbol for violence which so easily spills over into the world outside, with the baying spectators (shown in grotesque close-ups of sadistic women chewing peanuts and hurling abuse at the loser) as perverse voyeurs throughout it all.

Other fight films that de-romanticized boxing in the same way included *Iron Man* with Jeff Chandler (1951), Tony Curtis in *The Square Jungle* in 1955, and Humphrey Bogart's final movie, *The Harder They Fall* (directed by Mark Robson in 1956) in which he played a press agent representing a contender in the corruption-ridden fight business. And 1962's *Requiem For A Heavyweight*, with Anthony Quinn as a veteran of the ring, took another look at the sleazy side of the so-called "noble sport." Directed by Ralph Nelson and adapted from his own television play by Rod Serling, the film's opening fight sequence with its shots from the fighter's point of view, slow-motion takes, and flashing camera bulbs would be echoed by Scorsese in *Raging Bull*.

All these films presented boxing in a far from attractive light. The promotional tagline for *Champion* read "This is the only sport in the world where two guys get paid for doing something they'd be arrested for if they got drunk and did it for nothing," while the hero's girlfriend in *The Set-Up* (played by Audrey Totter) wryly comments "I want a man ... not a human punching bag!" Conversely, most of the main protagonists were cast in a sympathetic light—except for *Champion*'s Kelly, who would have more in common with *Raging Bull*'s Jake La Motta in that respect.

As well as the fictional fight movies, often using the ring as a stage to play out broader psychological and social issues, there were a number of (mostly insubstantial) biographical films based on boxers' careers. They included the 1890s-set *Gentleman Jim* (1942) with Errol Flynn as Gentleman Jim Corbett, another period piece *The Great John L.* (1945) about John L. Sullivan, and *The Joe Louis Story* (1953), which intercut real (black-and-white) footage with a dramatization of the great heavyweight's life. But the most celebrated, and rightfully so, was *Somebody Up There Likes Me*, starring Paul Newman as Jake La Motta's old street pal Rocky Graziano. Directed by Robert Wise (who also made *The Set-Up*), the 1956 movie did much to launch Newman's screen career.

## Black-and-white memories

All the pictures mentioned above, and most other boxing films of the era, were made in black and white. Not only was it the age of the monochrome movie, but for the *noir* ambience of the classics of the genre it was the "natural" option.

By the time *Raging Bull* was made, on the other hand, the overwhelming majority of commercial films were made in color. Indeed, it had become more expensive to shoot film using black-and-white stock. The notable films of the period made in monochrome, including *The Last Picture Show* (1971) and Woody's Allen's *Manhattan* (1979), were few and far between. And in that same decade, 1976's hugely successful *Rocky* and its 1979 sequel *Rocky II*, plus *Fat City* in 1972 and the 1970 Jack Johnson biopic *The Great White Hope*, were all boxing epics made in color. As well as his feeling that boxing was a "black-and-white" subject (and a concern that color stock was subject to fading) Scorsese made the choice for *Raging Bull* to distance it from these other, less "dark" and more upbeat fight films of the period.

Scorsese also wanted to achieve a more documentary "newsreel" feel in the film, again recalling the cinema of his youth, as well as the grainy black-and-white of the newspaper photography of the 1940s. As *Raging Bull* cinematographer Michael Chapman would explain, "The Forties were the great days of press photography, like the *New York Daily News* and *Life* magazine and photojournalism in the grand manner that we no longer have." Chapman was delighted to shoot in black and white: "I associate boxing with black and white, because of the pictures you saw in *Life* magazine, and the old newsreels, and the Friday night fights which was a staple of television in the Forties and Fifties, it was all black and white. And I'd never shot a movie in black and white and always wanted to, so I said 'yes, I'd love it.' "

As Scorsese told his backers when making the case for a black-and-white picture, "We had the idea of making the film look like a tabloid, like the *Daily News*, like Weegee photographs"—Weegee being the legendary news photographer who chronicled the often grim side of New York City in the Forties and Fifties.

Among films influencing *Raging Bull*, Scorsese has referred to two that had a specific bearing on his decision to shoot in black and white. They were *The Sweet Smell Of Success* (1957), Alexander Mackendrick's brutally frank study of corruption in the media, and *Night And The City* (1950), a London-set thriller by Jules Dassin starring Richard Widmark as a no-good hustler involved in the wrestling business.

### Hardboiled Hollywood

One of the few boxing scenes from another movie that Scorsese would acknowledge as directly influential was a short (sixty-seven second) sequence in John Ford's *The Quiet Man* (1952), in which John Wayne as an ex-boxer recalls in flashback the night he killed a man in the ring. In an otherwise non-boxing film, we suddenly see close-ups of faces and details—the trainer, a doctor, photographers, a towel being placed over the dead man's face—in a dream-like style that would be echoed in the fight sequences of the Scorsese film. He would also say that it was the only time a fight scene (albeit after the actual combat is over) shot in color impressed him: "When Wayne looks down and realizes he's killed his opponent ... I'll never forget the vibrance of his emerald green trunks."

Unlike *The Quiet Man*, however, a Technicolor romance about an Irish-American returning to the quaint village of his forefathers in the "old country," most of the films Scorsese cited as influences on *Raging Bull* were, though not always fight films, certainly of the *film noir* genus.

John Garfield, the chief protagonist in 1947's *Body and Soul*, would appear again the following year in *Force of Evil*, a film which made a major impact on Scorsese. Written and directed by Abraham Polonsky (who had also written *Body and Soul*), it's now regarded as a *noir* classic, the story of two brothers involved from opposing standpoints in the gangster-driven numbers racket.

What impressed Scorsese, as well as the tension between the two brothers, with one in the pay of the racketeers and the other fighting them, was the stylized verse-like dialogue in which Polonsky dispensed with punctuation and made great play of constant repetition. After Scorsese showed De Niro *Body And Soul*, the actor watched *Force Of Evil* which he said he found more interesting, given that the numbers scam was still rife in New York. The director would acknowledge the high regard in which he held the picture when he later included it in a series of films on videotape called "Martin Scorsese Presents."

Henry Hathaway's *Kiss of Death* (1947) was another seminal *film noir* which Scorsese identified with, describing it as "Twentieth Century Fox under the Italian Neo-Realist influence." It was shot largely on location, giving it a stark authenticity usually lacking in studio-based productions, and represented the screen debut of Richard Widmark as a sinister, giggling psychopath. The central character, played by Victor Mature, is an ex-con who goes straight by testifying against his cell-mate Widmark, but who is a marked man when the guy he's betrayed unexpectedly goes free. It explores a classic *noir* theme of a man being unable to escape his past, despite his attempt at redemption. It's a theme Scorsese would address again and again.

As in all his work, being cinema-literate to the point of obsession, Scorsese references many other films in *Raging Bull*. The most obvious is Elia Kazan's *On The Waterfront* (1954); not just in the soliloquy in the dressing room mirror, where Jake recites Brando's "I could have been a contender" speech, but in the whole premise of the movie following the aftermath of a boxer's time in the ring.

The central characters in both films have sins to redeem and demons to exorcise. For Brando's Terry Malone it's his inadvertent involvement in the killing of a fellow longshoreman and refusal to tell the authorities who the culprits are; for Jake it's his life of gratuitous violence towards others and the way he has treated those closest to him—his wife and brother. Terry finds redemption in finally facing his real enemies: not the authorities but the gangsters who will resort to murder in order to protect their grip on the docks and its lucrative cargos. Jake likewise faces his public, not in the confrontation of the boxing ring where violence is the only language, but in the equally candid arena of his stand-up club routine where he quotes from a wealth of literary sources in his nightly confessional.

In a 1996 appreciation of the director Samuel Fuller, Scorsese drew attention to one of the fight scenes in *Raging Bull* which he had based on a sequence from Fuller's *Steel Helmet* (1951), a ruggedly realistic account of men at war and one of the finest films set in the Korean conflict. And against the far more claustrophobic backdrop of a mental institution, Fuller's masterpiece *Shock Corridor* provided Scorsese with another inspiration for *Raging Bull*, the use of color in an otherwise black-and-white movie.

In the 1963 film, about a journalist who gets himself admitted to an asylum in order to solve the murder of an inmate, short color sequences were used to represent the disturbed mental condition of various characters. In Scorsese's picture, the tranquility of home movies shown in color contrasts with the grim reality of the rest of Jake La Motta's life.

While revisiting classic films of the past, Scorsese also took in some live action as part of his research for *Raging Bull*. The first bout he attended—he'd never been to a boxing match before—was with Walter Bernstein and Brian De Palma at Madison Square Garden, where he sketched various impressions of the scene. They were sitting way up at the back, and Bernstein had to talk him through the five fights that night as he found it hard to tell what was happening. He would recall that the first thing he drew was the blood-soaked sponge. It was being dipped in the water to sponge the young boxer between rounds, the blood running down the fighter's back as we would eventually see it do in stark slow-motion black and white.

For his next visit to a fight, also at Madison Square Garden, he had a seat in the third row, accompanied by Jake La Motta. This time the proximity to the ring allowed for an altogether more physical experience—"I could feel the sense of the blows, and how fast they were moving … then they were taking the first guy out, he'd lost, he was knocked out"—and the image that struck him most was of the defeated boxer's blood dripping from the ring rope: "I said to myself this sure didn't have anything to do with sport." The image would be reflected in the final shot of La Motta's last fight with Sugar Ray Robinson in *Raging Bull*.

# contenders

## The casting of Raging Bull

The casting of Robert De Niro as Jake La Motta was a *fait accompli*. It was the actor who had approached Scorsese in the first place with the original book, and proposed from the start that they could turn it into a movie with himself in the lead part. The other roles, however, particularly those of Jake's brother Joey and his second wife Vickie, were not so immediately filled.

Much as he was the driving force in kick-starting the film in the first place, De Niro was as pro-active as the director in seeking out likely candidates for the main supporting roles. Even before Scorsese had finally confirmed that they would be going ahead with *Raging Bull*, De Niro had been researching the project, including visiting Jake La Motta's ex-wife Vickie in Florida where she lived with her daughter Stephanie. Over several trips there (the first being when Mardik Martin was still involved in the project) he would talk over her life with La Motta and watch home movies—which Scorsese would later reconstruct in the movie. Likewise, while he and Scorsese were developing the script after their sojourn in St. Martin, De Niro was on the look-out for new faces who might play the parts of Vickie and Joey La Motta.

### Finding Joey

*The Death Collector* was a low-budget 1976 Mafia action thriller variously known as *Family Enforcer, The Collector*, and

*The Enforcer*. It did little at the box office, and certainly nothing to enhance the reputation of its director Ralph De Vito or lead players Joseph Cortese and Lou Criscuolo. De Niro came across the film on late-night television, and was immediately struck by the diminutive but dynamic actor playing the third main part, that of Joe, an enforcer for the Mob's debt-collecting; the actor's name was Joe Pesci.

Born in Newark, New Jersey on February 9 1943, Pesci was a child actor who began his radio career at the age of four. At five he was appearing on Broadway, and by 1953 he had a regular spot on the television variety series *Star Time Kids*. In the 1960s acting took a back seat in favor of music; he started what he hoped would be a singing career under the name of Joe Ritchie, and released an album entitled *Little Joe Sure Can Sing*. He was also playing guitar with several bands, including "Twist" specialists Joey Dee and The Starliters, and even formed a vaudeville-style nightclub comedy act with his friend Frank Vincent (who would also end up with a part in *Raging Bull*).

In fact it was an early link-up with Joey Dee that marked Pesci's first part in a film, an uncredited role as a nightclub dancer in 1961's *Hey, Let's Twist*, an exploitation movie cashing in on the dance craze which Dee was central to in his residency at New York's famed Peppermint Lounge. It was another fifteen years before Pesci appeared in another movie, *The Death Collector*, and when that bombed he returned to his native New Jersey and started managing an Italian restaurant in the Bronx, with no intention of getting back into the entertainment business.

As soon as he saw *The Death Collector* on television, De Niro felt Pesci could be perfect as Joey, and told Scorsese. When he got "the call" from the star actor and prestigious director, via casting director Cis Corman, Pesci said he didn't want to go back into movies "unless I get a part that proves I'm good." After going through the whole proposal over dinner, De Niro assured him that the part of Joey La Motta was a good role, though not necessarily a great role. Whatever, the idea sounded good enough for Pesci to attend a couple of readings: "I had no career, I had given up on acting ... I was a child actor since five, so even though I had given up on acting and didn't want anything to do with it anymore, the prospect of doing a movie with those two was exciting to me."

And the prospect of Pesci playing Joey was equally stimulating for Scorsese and De Niro, who said "He was just too special to not use him." It would mark the beginning of a hugely successful career as one of Hollywood's leading character actors.

Pesci recalls with amusement how in the course of making the film he would meet the real Joey La Motta. The actor was intent on studying the way La Motta walked, talked, and so on, "rather than using too much of myself." But on this occasion, it was his subject who looked *him* up and down from head to toe, walking around, seemingly assessing this guy who was going to play him in a movie. Eventually Pesci said to him, "Well they tried to get Robert Redford to play you but he was busy, so I'm playing you."

### Cathy Moriarty

When word got round Hollywood that Scorsese and De Niro were looking for an actress to play La Motta's second wife Vickie, there was no shortage of willing contenders for the role. In his biography of Robert De Niro, author John Baxter tells how, embarrassingly, Jodie Foster's mother even sent Scorsese photographs of her teenage daughter in a bikini when she heard that the role required Vickie to wear a swimsuit in some scenes.

But both De Niro and Scorsese were seeking an unknown, even someone with little experience, who could bring freshness and spontaneity to the role. Joe Pesci would provide the answer to what they were looking for, when he suggested Cathy Moriarty, an attractive seventeen-year-old blonde whose picture he'd seen flashed onto the wall of a local disco, and who subsequently visited his restaurant from time to time. A native New Yorker, Moriarty was born in the Bronx in November 1960 and raised in Westchester. She had virtually no acting experience when Scorsese and De Niro approached her. She confessed that all she'd done was some parts in high school (from which she was about to graduate), and was working to save up enough money to go to acting school.

After Cis Corman called her a couple of times to do a reading, the casting director told her she wanted her to meet "two gentlemen" who she referred to as Bob and Marty. In fact Moriarty had not even heard of De Niro, by then one of the leading names in Hollywood.

But her deep, sensual voice and mature demeanor convinced the two right away that she would be perfect for the part. "She had a composure, which I didn't know if it was either total confidence or complete panic which she was covering …" Scorsese remembers, "in either case it was good, because if it was panic then she could have fooled me."

Soon after they did a real screen test with her. A full crew was there, and Moriarty didn't realize all the people standing around were actually doing a job, so when Scorsese shouted "Action!" she just stood there, looking around, waiting for everyone to leave. "Cathy, you OK?" "Yeah, I'm just waiting for everybody to leave …" "Cathy, they're not leaving." But she sailed through the test, even when De Niro threw in some improvized lines.

On account of their discovery's totally "amateur" status, Scorsese and Cis Corman had to persuade the all-powerful Screen Actor's Guild that she was the only one for the job. Apparently Corman laid out ten pictures of Moriarty alongside ten of Vickie La Motta in front of the SAG executive, who were convinced immediately. Moriarty then had months of coaching by both De Niro and Scorsese. She would later compare it to having singing lessons from Pavarotti—"Robert De Niro and Martin Scorsese were so exceptionally loving to me and so concerned and so caring that I will always be grateful to them."

## New faces

In keeping with Scorsese's approach to casting in many of his other movies, most of the names further down the credits were almost as new to films as Moriarty. Frank Vincent, who plays the small-time Mob lieutenant Salvy Batts, was Joe Pesci's old show-biz partner and had his movie debut beside Pesci in *The Death Collector*—*Raging Bull* being only his second feature. "I had done one independent film before *Raging Bull*. I wasn't an 'actor' actor, I was trying to pursue that."

Pesci suggested he went for an audition for the part of Salvy. Joe joined him at the audition, which comprized the scene where the two are walking down the street. The whole thing was improvized, and two days later Vincent got a call for a screen test. When that was done, he was traveling from San Diego to Las Vegas when he decided to call Cis Corman, who simply said, "You got the job."

For Frank Adonis, who played Salvy's sidekick Patsy, *Raging Bull* was also his second credited film (after a part in 1978's *The Eyes Of Laura Mars*), while it marked the debut of Joseph Bono, who plays Salvy's other crony Guido.

Frank Topham, listed as a technical adviser, also had a small acting credit as Toppy, and it was his only film part ever. Perhaps surprisingly, Lori Anne Flax who plays La Motta's hard-done-by first wife Irma in just two (but totally riveting) scenes, has also never been credited with another film, before or since. And Martin Scorsese's father Charles, who featured memorably with his wife in the *Italianamerican* documentary, made his acting debut in *Raging Bull* as Mob chief Tommy Como's cousin Charlie—the first of ten movie parts (eight in films directed by his son) before his death in 1993.

While casting the movie, Cis Corman immersed herself in the world of boxing, talking to fighters, trainers, ring announcers, and such in her hunt for players of the smaller parts, with real referees and all of Jake La Motta's opponents in the ring being played by actual boxers who De Niro would meet when training for his role. In certain circumstances, Scorsese felt, real people brought something extra to a film that no actor could.

Scorsese got a certain amount of criticism from some actors for bringing so many (what they regarded as) "non-actors" into his films, with complaints that he was taking work away from "legit" members of the profession. But neither he nor De Niro ever saw it that way.

# gloves off

## The making of the movie

From the start, De Niro made it plain he wasn't going to portray the older, overweight Jake La Motta wearing body padding or a fat suit, so it was decided to shoot the film in two sections. The fight scenes and "early" sequences were shot first, then production shut down for a couple of months while the actor put on sixty pounds in order to become the latter-day Jake. But before a single camera rolled, Robert De Niro, with typical dedication to the character he was about to play, decided he had to learn to box.

### Sparring partners

In the course of research, De Niro, and later Scorsese, got to know Jake La Motta well, and the actor started taking boxing lessons with the ex-champ at New York's famous Gramercy Gym on East 14$^{th}$ Street. For several weeks he and Jake would spar in the ring, supervized by Al Silvani, who had coached La Motta years before and was also Sylvester Stallone's trainer for the *Rocky* movies. They fought hundreds of rounds together, a half hour every day, and La Motta was a tireless perfectionist as far as De Niro's style in the ring was concerned: "Whaddya want people to think—that I was some kind of jerk?"

De Niro—who wore a headguard and mouthpiece when sparring with Jake—got so proficient that he once broke one of La Motta's teeth. And as soon as he was ready he sparred through three genuine fights in a Brooklyn boxing arena, winning on points in two.

It was during De Niro's sparring period that the decision was made to film *Raging Bull* in black and white. He and Scorsese had made some 8mm color footage of the gym work-outs with La Motta and co, which they watched in the director's 57$^{th}$ Street apartment in the company of Michael Powell (the great British director who they'd known since the early Seventies and whose work Scorsese admired). Scorsese knew there was something about the sparring images, projected on the back of a door, that simply wasn't quite right. Suddenly Powell said, "The gloves are wrong, the color of the gloves," and Scorsese realized immediately he was right— they were bright red, whereas in the period of the film they would have been oxblood, maroon, or even just black. Scorsese admitted to being "obsessed with color" for most of his movies, but right there when Powell made his observation, they decided to shoot *Raging Bull* in black and white.

There was also the issue of the preservation of old films. Color film stocks at that time tended to fade very badly, and Scorsese was very concerned about the fate of the movies he'd already made. They knew if they shot it in black and white it wouldn't fade, so that was another reason to go down the monochrome road.

Principal photography on *Raging Bull* began in April 1979, starting with the first fight scenes, which (set in Madison Square Garden) were shot in a Los Angeles warehouse. All the actual fight sequences were filmed there or in the studio, with extraneous shots of the crowd, of the fighters climbing in and out of the ring, and so on, being filmed in a legendary but still-used LA boxing arena, the Olympic Auditorium. The sequences in the ring were carefully choreographed by Scorsese, De Niro and cinematographer Michael Chapman like dance routines, with diagrams of feet and arrows showing the actors exactly where to move, as Chapman would describe: "Each shot was drawn out in great detail, almost like Arthur Murray, those weird dance steps they used to draw on the floor. We did that." Likewise each camera angle, every camera movement, and the precise distance of framing was carefully mapped out with same meticulousness.

In fact, the origination of this "choreography" was back in the sparring ring, in the nine fight scenes which De Niro, Jake La Motta, and stunt coordinator Jimmy Nickerson had worked up. They got Scorsese down to the gym to show him what they had in mind. De Niro got in the ring with Nickerson, and they went through the moves of each fight, each two or three minutes long. Scorsese admitted to being stunned: "I realized it was going to take an extraordinary amount of effort to do what I wanted to do, but I didn't exactly know what I wanted to do yet. In fact I was so stunned I couldn't react, and I just sat there." At one point, De Niro climbed out of the ring to see what the problem was, asking him point-blank: "Are you paying attention? 'Cos we're killing ourselves in there!"

Assuring De Niro he was OK, Scorsese got to thinking how, if he wasn't careful, shooting this was going to take years. He had to design it so it would work efficiently, and with that in mind took home a black-and-white video of the fight moves he'd seen demonstrated.

He decided to make a series of drawings and diagrams with notes for each shot, just like he'd done for the musical numbers in *New York, New York*.

In the fight sequences, just one camera was to be used, not the usual three, four, or five. Everything was to be intercut later—the impact of each shot coming out in the selecting process in the editing room. He devized what he referred to as "a sense of how to coach them in boxing as choreography, as music really, just as music." Michael Chapman felt that the analogy with dance sequences went even deeper, each fight's characteristics being reflected in the movement—one fight being a tango, another a foxtrot, and so on.

Scorsese wanted everything in the ring to be filmed with one camera. Inspired by James Wong Howe's hand-held shots in the 1947 boxing movie *Body and Soul*, he had Chapman right in the middle of the action, taking the place of the opponent as he shot the fighter coming forward, raining punches towards the camera. Thus, in many ways, the camera (as an extension of Scorsese and Chapman's vision for the film) became the sparring partner with the actors, not the actors with each other.

**Filming the fights**
Details of what was going on outside the ring are also seen from the insider's, that is the boxer's, point of view. The flashing cameras, animated newsmen, the faces of fans relishing the violence, a fracas that breaks out in the crowd at the end of the first fight sequence—all are shown from the perspective of the combatants; and as viewers we're on the inside looking out.

Scorsese made a positive decision to "stay away" from the audience, in other words to stay inside the ropes most of the time. Looking at other boxing movies or newsreels, he couldn't see what appreciation there could be of the boxers' emotions shot from outside the ring looking in. He realized, not being a fight aficionado, there were objective things about boxing skills—the beautiful moves and so on—that he didn't recognize, that could doubtless be best viewed at a distance.

But in order to get *inside* the fighters' minds, the only time the camera is outside the ring during actual fight sequences is when Jake is not trying (when he throws the fight), or in a sequence (as in a fight with Sugar Ray Robinson) where he's playing possum. Then the camera is outside the ropes, low down at the level of the canvas; a front-row perspective which is sometimes just a view of the boxers' boots. But as soon as Jake starts swinging some hooks, the crane-held camera sweeps us through the ropes, around the fighters, and back into the ring.

Various techniques were employed by Scorsese and Chapman to enhance each fight sequence with its own individual characteristics. Slow-motion filmed through long lenses, for instance, added to a sense of the increasing claustrophobia during one of La Motta's battles with Sugar Ray Robinson where he loses to his rival. The image was distorted by putting a flame in front of the lens as they filmed, giving a hazy "mirage" effect as Jake's own perception of what's going on gets more sluggish.

Scorsese would even change the size and shape of the ring to enhance what he wanted to convey about Jake's emotional state. The first time we see him knock down Sugar Ray in the ring is large and sweeping, the lighting is bright, reflecting the elation of the moment. But, later, when Sugar Ray defeats him, the ring—as well as being dark and smoky—is smaller, enveloping its occupants almost like a prison cell. And when De Niro sits down in his corner, there's a rope interrupting our view of his face. One of La Motta's more straightforward contests, on the other hand, is shown with just opera music on the soundtrack, nothing distracting from the seeming inevitability of victory.

Other sequences use devices such as stop-frames, extreme close-ups, and jump-cut editing to convey the dynamic of the combat in an impressionistic, sometimes almost surreal way. But all the time, Scorsese retains a sense of "realism" in his portrayal of the action, despite the images themselves being highly contrived.

Michael Chapman would describe how they "choreographed" sequences of the ringside photographer's flashbulbs going off around the boxers, sometimes shooting them so as to achieve the effect of hypnotic strobe lighting. He felt the flashes were highly effective both as a punctuation to the drama in the ring, and in "casting behind and around the fighters an aura of light," the latter at times reminiscent of religious iconography.

One of the most stunning uses of the flashbulb imagery comes right at the beginning of the movie, in the credit sequence, where Jake is shot in slow motion in the ring, with a series of flashes going off in the background. Michael Chapman was actually taking the flashes, dressed in black velour so he wouldn't be visible, shooting and reloading in the dark, then being led to the next position as he could hardly see being covered from head to toe. They were using vintage Speed Graphic cameras from the 1940s, with very old flashbulbs that had a slow rate of decay. Scorsese and Chapman had found that modern flashbulbs are so fast that they often don't show up when photographed, whereas with the slower bulbs they were able to achieve a spectacular effect in slow motion.

The impact of the fight scenes as Scorsese envisaged them could only be achieved by painstaking editing, and in that task he was aided by Thelma Schoonmaker (who was to win an Oscar for the editing). After the awards ceremony, she would modestly insist that it should have gone to the director; they both knew it was won for the fight sequences more than anything else, and according to Schoonmaker they were entirely "Marty's" creation, which she helped realize. The editor recalled that producer Irwin Winkler protested that they couldn't mix the film inch by inch, which Scorsese insisted was exactly what *was* going to happen. As a consequence, post-production, which was scheduled to take seven weeks, ended up taking six months.

On at least one occasion, despite Scorsese's elaborate storyboards laying out exactly what he wanted, the edited footage did not turn out the way he had first envisaged. It was during the sequence of the final beating that Jake takes from Sugar Ray Robinson, where the Bronx Bull refuses to go down. As director and editor worked on the scene, they discovered that what Schoonmaker called "the kinetic flow of the actual images" dictated a different flow than that planned for, so they spent a long time changing the shots around to get it right. Even though the storyboards were vitally important, in that particular sequence they found it necessary to "violate" them.

So precise were the director's requirements for each shot that he realized that the fight sequences could only be filmed as he wanted to in a studio environment, and, as Schoonmaker realized, with just the one camera which would be his "eye." "He didn't want five cameramen shooting something in a way that he had not designed, and so Marty knew that the camerawork that he was going to do would be so complicated that he would have to be in a studio where he could have maximum control with the lighting, the size of the ring, and so on, so he decided to do it all in a very intense period of shooting in a studio environment." The results often involved what film academic Todd Berliner would describe as "visual absurdity"—an illogical, out-of-step series of images that didn't make any literal sense if "read" one after another, but impacted as a whole (much in the same way that the words of a poem don't have to necessarily form a "narrative" in order to convey what the writer wants).

In this way, a shot of a fighter delivering a right-hand punch is followed by an image of his opponent being struck by what is clearly a left blow to the face. Or an uninterrupted series of punches is shown without the pauses that would naturally punctuate the action. The sheer rapidity of the cuts and the disoriented nature of their sequencing was, according to Scorsese, aimed at conveying the fighter's subjective view of the violence, "not a matter of literally translating what Jake sees and hears."

One sequence that was directly related to a fight scene, but not depicting the combat as such, was the spectacular tracking shot tracing La Motta's walk from the dressing room to the ring prior to his middleweight championship bout with Marcel Cerdan. In its uninterrupted flow it contrasts sharply with the frantic collage of images of the fight itself, a cinematic *tour de force* in which Scorsese and Michael Chapman evoke the whole gladiatorial theatricality that preludes the violence about to be enacted in the ring.

For this sequence Chapman utilized the newly developed steady-cam camera-stabilizing system, whereby tracking shots could be achieved with a hand-held camera (they used an ultra-lightweight Arriflex) without the use of actual tracks or dollies. Starting with De Niro's Jake warming up in his basement dressing room, punching his brother who is wearing a protector, the camera backs away from him, staying ahead of them as they walk through the corridors that lead up into the arena. Here there was a crowd of 2,000 extras, the most Scorsese was allowed to use in the film, and as Jake and his entourage enter high up in the auditorium the cameraman pauses to let them pass, and then starts following them down towards the ring, stepping onto a cherry-picker crane that brings him up into a high overhead shot as De Niro enters the ring.

The transition that takes place as the camera switches from a front view of Jake to a following position is crucial to the whole sequence. In the privacy of the "backstage" shots, Jake faces us and dominates the picture, then as the camera moves behind him and trails further behind, we become part of the crowd as he all but disappears into the throng. Finally, the camera sweeps up and over as we take a more "objective" view of Jake's arrival before becoming a part of the action within the ring itself.

Thelma Schoonmaker remembers how Scorsese's preferred take of the tracking shot was rendered completely unusable when the camera was damaged: "The first thing I had to do was to call and tell Marty he had lost his preferred take. Fortunately he had an excellent other take which we ended up using." The editor still thinks so highly of the shot that she uses it as an example whenever she teaches classes.

The fight scenes were all shot in Los Angeles, and were initially scheduled to take five weeks. However, with the meticulous shot-by-shot technique adopted by Scorsese (which he himself would describe as "laborious"), the process stretched to twice that amount of time. In fact the ten weeks devoted to the fight scenes was half of the time that it took to shoot the entire picture, even though the fights only occupy less than twenty minutes of the two-hour-plus movie. Producers Winkler and Chartoff, who in other circumstances might have balked at the extra time being devoted to the fights, were happy to let things ride when they could see how good the results were. And the studio caused them no problems. According to Winkler, because United Artists were preoccupied with Michael Cimino's grossly over-budget *Heaven's Gate* "they kind of left us alone."

**Improvizing**
What Scorsese describes as "the dramatic scenes," meaning those away from the boxing arena, were shot in both New York and Los Angeles. Much has been made of the improvized nature of the actors' performances in this and other Scorsese films, but what you see on the screen was already carefully set in "tablets of stone." The improvization

would come in rehearsal, where Scorsese would transcribe everything they decided to use, that then being what Pesci calls "The Bible" from which Marty wouldn't let them divert unless something really sensational cropped up while they were shooting.

One of Scorsese's techniques to stimulate improvization was to introduce an element of surprise into the action. A case in point was the scene where a violent argument between Jake and his first wife Irma is interrupted by Joey. The elder brother's presence calms things down, but Jake's still in a volatile mood as his wife shuts herself in the bedroom. Then, just as Joey is attempting to talk him out of his anger, Jake explodes again as someone shouts from the street for these "animals" to keep quiet.

After screaming out of the window—"You're an animal"—almost to the world at large it seems, Jake returns his attention into the room, encouraging Joey to punch him in the face. At first his brother refuses, then hits him with his fist wrapped in a towel. "Harder, harder" Jake urges, then "Take it off," so Joey finishes the pummeling bare-knuckle style. It's as if Jake seeks punishment, in this case to redeem the guilt of how he treats his wife, and, we can surmise, the world out there. A world that re-enters the action, again via the open window, but this time we hear not a vocal neighbor but the riffs of a big band on a nearby radio, which take over the soundtrack as the scene fades.

The shouted complaint from outside is pivotal to the scene, separating Jake's anger with his wife from his seeking redemption (by asking his own brother to hurt him), yet its introduction was the result of an improvizatory "surprise" on

Scorsese's part. They had been shooting the scene with De Niro and Pesci again and again (each time it seemed to be getting better), when Scorsese had the idea of putting one of the prop men outside in the tenement alley, suddenly shouting up at Jake and Joey. De Niro immediately responded, taking his dialogue into an angry tirade shouted out of the window before returning to the scripted lines with Pesci. It seems Scorsese had deliberately chosen a guy who could "motivate" De Niro, in that he had the kind of personality that could easily wind the actor up—and succeeded in exactly the way the director intended.

Scorsese also wanted to evoke the whole atmosphere of the New York tenements (like the district he grew up in) with the sounds—music, family arguments, food cooking, kids playing—that wafted in and out of the windows.

The element of surprise also came into play when Pesci's Joey suddenly attacks mobster Salvy (played by Frank Vincent) in a nightclub. The two actors were old buddies, of course, and Vincent later admitted that he didn't know if he would have done the shot had it been with someone different. He and Pesci worked through the scene meticulously, to get the timing exactly right, as one moment Joey is exchanging words with Salvy, the next he's exploding into violence. But when it came to the actual shoot, none of the extras sitting at the neighboring tables had been told what was about to happen. When Pesci suddenly turned on Vincent, there were genuine screams as some thought the fight was "for real"—real or not, they scattered out of the way as fists flew and glasses crashed. Even the table falling over was "improvized" in that it wasn't planned to happen, but it all made for a totally realistic scene.

Equally unplanned was the dialogue between Jake and his future wife Vickie after they've just been introduced by Joey. The two talk through a chainlink fence in a scene inspired by the meeting of Marlon Brando and Eva Marie Saint in *On The Waterfront*, but none of the lines that De Niro and Cathy Moriarty deliver were previously in the script. Moriarty was amused after the film was released by how her nervous comment through the fence—"Nice car"—became a celebrated line, people saying to her "Say it again Cathy, say it again … 'nice car'…" Suddenly they had what she'd describe as "this lovely little scene," as Jake, in unusually tender mode, asks almost shyly, "You wanna go for a ride?" to which Vickie responds "Can you give me a minute? I just have to change."

Both De Niro and Scorsese felt that Moriarty's lack of experience was beneficial in many ways. She had a natural instinct for interaction with her fellow actors, even though sometimes the going could get tough, especially at the improvizatory stage. The scene in which Jake accuses Vickie of sleeping with Joey—"Did you fuck my brother?", "Why did you fuck Joey?"—was particularly harrowing, as she backs off and locks herself in the bathroom while he threatens her and she refuses to open the door. The next moment, Jake smashes the door off its hinges and onto the floor of the narrow bathroom. Moriarty wasn't expecting this, and described it as one of the most frightening moments she'd experienced. When she made light of it, someone said "Cathy, we only have six doors, so we only have to do this six times."

She continues to get him increasingly angry by taunting him. In this way, Moriarty explained, she was "supporting" De Niro in a very difficult scene, giving him something to respond to, to channel the anger. The scene moves to Vickie following Jake down the street, as he goes to attack his brother, hitting him first before he knocks her down onto the ground, delivering a blow which is hidden from our view by a parked car. Moriarty felt that, right through their relationship, Vickie takes Jake on "in her own way," but that she did sincerely love him, and understood him, perhaps uniquely. She loved him in a way that prevented her from blaming him for *everything* all of the time, sensing it wasn't all *just* his fault. Scorsese, too, perhaps reflecting his basic dislike of boxing, could see how the participants were not necessarily to blame one hundred percent for the way they acted out of the ring, given how they were expected (and paid) to behave within it.

Cathy Moriarty, despite her inexperience, warmed to the role of Vickie—and the "Method" influence of her prime tutor De Niro cannot be overestimated in this respect—to the extent that she was determined to *become* Vickie in many ways. In the 2005 DVD release of the movie, she recalls in one of the "bonus" documentaries how she managed to get the hair right with the aid of Jean Burt Reilly, who sadly died before the film was released. "She was a hairdresser who had worked with Marilyn Monroe, so I used to love to go to see Jean because I would get all the great stories." Reilly set her hair with corn syrup applied to the ends: "Only problem was, bees in the summer used to circle my head." When they were shooting the pool scene, Reilly would send her home with pin-curlers in her hair—"I think it was just to make sure I didn't go out that night."

## Blood brothers

The relationship between Jake and Joey La Motta is central to the whole structure of *Raging Bull*. Through Jake's increasing suspicion of the one person who has probably been closer to him throughout his life than anyone, we have a perfect illustration of his growing paranoia and jealousy.

The scene where this is spelled out, with Jake standing by the television set and Joey sitting down, was the longest in the script, covering seven pages or so. But the paranoia that emerges as Jake needles his brother about Vickie was achieved by very carefully planned dialogue, to which virtually no improvization was added—the tension behind the words escalating with each line.

"I'm your brother, you're supposed to believe me, don't you trust me?"

"No, I don't "

"Oh you don't … that's nice …"

"I don't trust you when it comes to her—I don't trust nobody."

The point where Jake actually says "You fucked my wife" to his brother was crucial, and De Niro went through it repeatedly with Pesci, trying to elicit what he and Scorsese felt was the right reaction. At one stage he said to Pesci, off camera, "You fucked your mother," and the latter's totally shocked reaction was the one they used.

Equally crucial is the scene at the end of the film where the brothers are reconciled. De Niro strikes a pathetic figure as the now-corpulent Jake begs his brother to "forgive and forget," Joey seeming initially embarrassed by this uncharacteristic show of affection. Knowing that the two actors had become close friends, Scorsese forbade them seeing each other for a while prior to shooting the scene, not wanting them to talk about it. The emotional impact on Pesci, listening to the begging for forgiveness, was all the more powerful.

## The weight

Robert De Niro had made it clear before the film started shooting that he wanted to play the latter-day Jake La Motta by putting on an extra sixty pounds or so, just like the boxer had, but in a matter of weeks. The producers thought it was a bad idea—apart from holding up the movie, it wasn't going to do the actor's health any good. They said they could use prosthetics, puff his face up and so on, but De Niro insisted he had to put on the weight to *become* the older Jake.

So production was put on hold, the entire crew being paid for about four months, while the actor—as Martin Scorsese would put it—"ate his way around Northern Italy and France." A great fan of Italian cuisine, De Niro embarked on a daunting regime of getting up at 6.30 every morning for breakfast at 7am, in order to digest his food before lunch, which he then needed to digest so he could look forward to a good dinner in the evening.

When he got back to the US, his weight had increased from around 150 pounds to 210-plus, and it was taking its toll. He was having trouble breathing, he couldn't bend to tie his shoelaces, and his voice had deepened into a gruff whisper. "I began to realize what a fat man goes through," De Niro later said. "You get rashes on your legs. Your legs scrape together."

He was not immediately recognizable when he arrived back in Hollywood—indeed Irwin Winkler didn't recognize him when he walked, smiling, into his office. Scorsese, concerned that De Niro couldn't carry on long like this—though the actor insisted he knew what he was doing—decided they should shoot the final scenes as quickly as possible, over seven or eight days. It was coming up to Christmas 1979.

The first time we see the bloated Jake in the film is by the poolside with his wife and children, when he announces to a reporter that he's retired from the fight game. "It's over for me. Boxing's over for me. I'm through. I'm tired of worryin' about weight all the time. That's all I used to think about was weight, weight, weight. After a while, you know, you realize other things in life. I mean, I'm very grateful. Boxing's been good to me: I've got a nice house, I've got three great kids, I've got a wonderful, beautiful wife—what more could I ask for?" The lines reflected Jake La Motta's conversations with De Niro when the ex-champ recalled how his big concern had always been "the weight" when he was fighting, and De Niro decided he wanted to experience that sensation of putting on all those pounds.

One of the most traumatic scenes in the film is undoubtedly the scene in the prison cell when Jake is faced with his own demons and there's no-one to lash out at; he's truly alone as he bashes his fist, and then his head, against the cell wall. The walls of the cell set were padded with a rubber cushioning then painted to look right, and the only light was the thin shafts of illumination that cut through the darkness. De Niro had told Scorsese how La Motta had demonstrated to him how he hit the wall, in a hotel room, and the director wanted to get it absolutely right—"That's the whole movie … that's what the film's about."

## Home movies

A fascinating feature of the film, particularly from the post-production point of view, was the inclusion of snatches of "home movies" of Jake and his family, shot in color. They were based on the real home movies that De Niro and Marty had watched in their research, all shot on a 16mm camera. Scorsese had commented that these gave a better picture of La Motta's actual life than *Raging Bull* did. He felt that through the smiling faces in the amateur films you could see the decay in the family, so to indicate a passage of time in *Raging Bull* he decided to replicate those old home movies, making them as much like Jake's as he could.

When they started shooting the "home movie" sequences—family get-togethers, weddings, and so on—a very basic problem became apparent: they were too professional. Michael Chapman found he couldn't frame the shots "badly" enough, he simply brought too much of an artist's eye to the process. Likewise when Scorsese tried, he was unable to make it look convincingly amateur. Eventually they got teamsters who were driving the trailers, who had no experience of wielding a movie camera whatsoever, to shoot the "home movie" footage.

Just some "wobbly" framing wasn't convincing enough, of course. They needed the footage to look worn—as if it had been lying around for a while. With that in mind they desaturated the color to give the correct faded effect that would have occurred over the years. Then Scorsese and

Schoonmaker cut in flash frames and segments from other footage, so the home movies looked as if they'd been broken and then spliced. Scorsese even went into the cutting room and—much to the horror of the negative cutter, who as Schoonmaker said "prides herself on never making a scratch on your negative"—scratched the negative so it looked damaged, as if it had been wrongly threaded some time.

With the rest of the movie being shot on black-and-white stock, the color footage had to be spliced in by hand, there in the lab, with the sound being mixed accordingly. Schoonmaker tells a funny story of how she was checking around movie theaters in the New York area, to see how the film was being projected and whether it was being shown properly, at the correct luminance, and so on. She went into one projection booth and introduced herself, only to find the projectionist spooling out all of the "home movie" sequence on to the floor. Asked by the shocked editor what he was doing, the projectionist explained that the lab had obviously made a mistake, they had cut in a color sequence from some other film.

### Sound and music

The soundtrack accompanying both the dramatic scenes and the fight images contained elements far removed from any "naturalistic" reality. While some of the sounds—crowds cheering and jeering, a radio commentary, the ringside bell—added authenticity to the boxing sequences, they were segued in with more alien effects to complement what could be termed the hyper-realism of the visual editing. And this was also the case with the non-fight scenes which comprized the majority of the film.

Initially, during the rough cuts, Scorsese applied his own fairly basic sound effects, but decided they weren't at all satisfactory. They brought in Frank Warner, who had worked on Spielberg's *Close Encounters Of The Third Kind* and with Scorsese on *Taxi Driver*, and together with Scorsese he went through the whole movie, scene by scene.

At the time, Warner had one of the biggest independent libraries, about a million feet on quarter-inch reels. He would watch a particular scene, then find something that would seem appropriate, and work on it on an almost micro basis, forward and reversing tiny bits of recording just to get little snippets here and there.

In one of the Sugar Ray Robinson fights, use was made of the sound of a drum banging, sometimes distorted, sometimes straight. It punctuates the other more chaotic sounds going around the ring and in the crowd in an almost ceremonial way. Among other devices the sound man employed were animal noises like the roar of a lion, the scream of an unidentified jungle creature, rifle shots, and even the sound of a tomato being squashed or a melon broken open. The distinctive trumpeting of an elephant accompanies an image of Jake coming in to hit an opponent; when he knocks Sugar Ray Robinson to the floor we hear a horse shuddering.

Frank Warner applied the same painstaking attention to the film as a whole. He would manipulate sounds by controlling their speed and direction to often mind-jarring effect. The pandemonium of shouting and screaming in the scene where Jake attacks Joey in his home, with the brothers' wives trying to pull him off, was accentuated by the addition of a surreal "screech" which Warner achieved by scraping ice against a pain of glass. Equally effective was the sound of the flashbulbs that explode effervescently. In order to achieve a staccato effect like a rapid series of gun shots, he overlaid the basic sound of a flashbulb with five or six other sounds, the origin of which he refused to reveal to Scorsese saying, "If I told you, all the magic would be gone."

Keeping his "tricks of the trade" to himself in this way was a matter of principal to Warner. At the end of any film he worked on, he would burn all the sound effects he created for that particular movie. Not so much to prevent others using them, his main motive in destroying his work was to make sure *he* didn't use them again, ensuring he came to a new project with a genuinely blank canvas. It was also a proprietary question as far as Warner was concerned. He felt that what he had created for a certain picture belonged to the director and producers of that picture. Destroying the sounds after completion meant he wouldn't—even minimally or unintentionally—replicate them elsewhere.

"One of the best things we did," Scorsese recalled, "was to drop the sound out completely at certain moments. Silence, then suddenly the punch goes flying—whack!" Warner has said: "The richest sound that I had to offer was silence," and there were key moments in the movie when he decided it would be more effective to take the sound away, then bring it back in—contrary to the usual convention of raising the sound at a crucial point in the action. A stunning example comes when Jake is taking a terrible beating from Sugar Ray Robinson, but refusing to go down. As Sugar Ray pulls away for a moment, incredulous that La Motta isn't giving up though he's clearly finished, the lights in the ring dim and the sound all but disappears, before rising to a crescendo when Robinson comes in for the kill.

The other major element on any Scorsese soundtrack is the music. This is usually not a written score as such—at least not as far as Scorsese's input is concerned—but rather the peppering of the action with sounds of the time and place, "background" music from jukeboxes, radios, etc. The director's great love, and detailed knowledge, of all kinds of popular music has ensured that his personal imprint is very much present on the soundtrack of many of his movies.

Throughout *Raging Bull* we hear the music of the era coming out of tenement windows, in the background in clubs and bars, from a radio by the poolside. "There's not a song in the background of the film that wouldn't have been played on the radio at that time," Scorsese recalled. But the actual theme music of the picture, if we can call it that, has a very different feel to it.

Scorsese relates how, when he was just a kid, an uncle gave him a ten-inch long player of "intermezzi"—operatic intermezzos—the sort of thing much loved by the older generation of Italian immigrants. Although he loved (and grew up on) 1940s pop singers, the big bands, and later rock'n'roll, one tune on the "high-brow" album always stuck in his mind—the Intermezzo from *Cavalleria Rusticana*, written in 1890 by the Italian Pietro Mascagni. By way of experiment, just to see how it worked, he and Thelma Schoonmaker tried putting the music on the opening shot of the film, under the credits with the first image of Jake La Motta, alone in the smoked-filled ring in his hooded leopard-skin robe. It worked perfectly.

The actual sound mixing, which was set to take eight weeks, eventually took twice that long. Scorsese slept in a trailer which he had pulled up to the back door of the sound stage, where they worked on the mix from eight in the morning to eight in the evening, seven days a week. Scorsese would describe the process thus: "It was really quite as intricate as the fight scenes. In fact the dramatic scenes were hard to do, but they were almost a vacation compared to the fight scenes and the mix."

When they were finally near to completing the mix, Irwin Winkler told him that the film was going to open on the Friday of the following week in New York, Los Angeles, and Toronto. They had to get a print up to Toronto by the Thursday at the latest, in order for the Canadian censors to see it; this meant they had a Sunday deadline for finishing the mix, to allow time for the final print to be processed in the lab. They agreed to wrap things up at midnight on the Sunday, but when the moment came to get the film to the lab, Scorsese wanted a little more time. He was concerned that in the scene at the Copacabana Club, you couldn't hear the words "Cutty Sark" as someone ordered a drink. Winkler agreed, you couldn't hear it, but so what? They'd been there seven days a week for months—"the guys are falling asleep at the mixing booth ... I can't hear anything, you can't hear anything, and it's gonna be, that's it, were gonna wrap." To which Scorsese replied angrily that if they wrapped right there and then, they could take his name off the film—it would no longer be a Martin Scorsese picture. They did wrap there and then, and Scorsese subsequently relented.

But the sound of any movie is only as good as the system that's playing it in the cinema, as Marty and Winkler found when they took a print of the film to New York. They were standing at the back of the theater at the first screening as the movie started. The sound was appalling, and Winkler asked the manager what was wrong with the sound system. The manager was taken aback: "What's wrong with the sound? I just went to Radio Shack and bought four new speakers at $59.95, and you're complaining about the sound?"

## The final cut

As with any motion picture—and this was particularly true of *Raging Bull*—the final essence of the film was achieved in the cutting room. In the first cut of the film, Jake La Motta's nightclub act was used throughout the narrative to introduce "flashbacks" to his younger days. This was Paul Schrader's original idea, along with the dressing room scenes "bookending" the film. Eventually, Scorsese and Thelma Schoonmaker decided they could effectively dispense with the multi-flashback idea—making the film just one complete flashback—by ripping out most of the "on-stage" footage and ending up with the rehearsal-in-the-mirror sequences to begin and end the movie. It was a structure that presented in a clearly defined context an otherwise open-ended narrative. It also made clear from the start (and confirmed at the finish) that this was a film concerning the way Jake La Motta felt about himself rather than a straightforward saga of a boxer's rise and fall.

Released in November 1980, although initially greeted with mixed reviews—Scorsese himself admits, "I didn't think

anybody was going to come and see the picture that much"—
*Raging Bull* went on to be considered one of the director's finest
works, some would say his masterpiece. It was certainly a
turning point in both his and Robert De Niro's creative
development, both as individual artists and as a collaborative
team.

# blow by blow

## A scene-by-scene commentary

With the film's title a splash of blood red on an otherwise grainy black-and-white image, the opening credit sequence of *Raging Bull* sets the mood of the film as De Niro's La Motta shadow boxes in a smoke-filled ring. With the hood on his leopard-skin robe obscuring his face as he moves in slow motion to the strains of the Intermezzo from *Cavalleria Rusticana*, he strikes an isolated figure in the arena. The world outside the ring is merely hinted at by the hazy impression of ringside spectators behind him, the soundless explosion of camera flashbulbs in the distance briefly illuminating the auditorium like mortar fire over a silent battlefield.

### That's entertainment!

The rest of the credits over the sequence are white, then, after a title card which reads *New York City 1964*, we're looking down a billboard outside the Barbizon Plaza Theater announcing "An Evening with Jake La Motta Tonight 8:30." Cutting to La Motta's dressing room, we see the overweight Jake rehearsing his act alone in front of the mirror, reciting some badly rhyming verse of his own invention interspersed with a snatch of Shakespeare: " 'A horse, a horse, my kingdom for a horse'—I haven't had a winner in six months," and so on. His monologue ends, "So gimme a stage, Where this bull here can rage, And though I can fight, I'd much rather recite, That's entertainment!" As he repeats "That's entertainment!" we're suddenly witnessing a rain of vicious blows to the face of a much younger man before another title card informs us: *Jake La Motta 1941.*

## First blood

The scene is a Cleveland bout early in La Motta's career, and a voice-over of an announcer tells us that so far he's been undefeated in the professional ring. We learn from his corner between rounds that his opponent, the black Jimmy Reeves, is winning on points and Jake needs a knock-out to win. Then, as the "Bronx Bull" is about to go in for the kill, our attention is distracted briefly by a fight breaking out simultaneously in the crowd. As we will see in Jake's life generally, violence isn't limited to the contests within the ring. In the first of many instances showing the gruesome reality of boxing, La Motta's relentless pummeling renders his opponent helpless, blood pouring from Reeves' eye as he goes down once, then twice, then three times, only to be "saved by the bell" as the fight finishes.

La Motta paces the ring in triumph, arms upraised to his supporters, as the announcer declares the "vanquished" Reeves the winner. The result, of course, has been fixed by the Mob, but it's a decision Jake won't accept as he refuses to leave the ring, and a riot breaks out in the crowd. Mayhem ensues as chairs are thrown into the ring, a woman is trampled underfoot, and the last we see is a long shot from up at the back, chaos engulfing the arena as an organist in the foreground of the picture vainly plays "The Star Spangled Banner."

## Bronx life

It's *The Bronx New York City 1941*, and Joe Pesci's Joey is walking to his brother Jake's apartment with Salvy (Frank Vincent), a small-time player in the local Mafia set-up. Salvy tells Joey how Jake will have to cooperate with the Mob if he's going to get a shot at a title, otherwise "he's gonna wind up fuckin' punch-drunk." Joey agrees, but clearly doesn't know whether he can persuade his volatile brother.

We get to see just how volatile Jake can be as the scene changes to inside the apartment, where he's bemoaning the fight decision to his clearly put-upon wife Irma, who's serving him dinner. He suddenly turns his anger towards her, shouting that she's overcooked his steak, whereupon the brow-beaten spouse slams the plate down on the table, take-it-or-leave-it style. Jake pushes the dinner table over in an eruption of domestic violence that is clearly nothing new in their marriage. Meanwhile, on the street outside Jake's apartment building, Joey is telling Salvy he'll try to talk to his brother about falling in with Salvy's mobster boss Tommy Como, "If he's in a good mood." When he gets upstairs he realizes this is certainly not the right time as he interrupts the frenzied quarrel. Just then someone shouts from the street below, complaining about the noise from "you animals," distracting Jake momentarily from the argument with his wife as he delivers a tirade from the window at his aggrieved neighbor.

Jake quietens down after that, calming things with his wife before telling his brother that he feels he'll never make it in the fight game on account of his small hands. Joey says that's ridiculous, then Jake challenges him to punch him in the jaw. At first his brother refuses, but after being taunted—

"Don't be a little faggot. Come on. Hit me."—wraps a towel round his hand and punches Jake in the face, again and again. An almost masochistic ritual ensues, with strong sexual undertones, as Jake tells Joey to take off the towel, slapping him to goad him some more. Joey hits him, bare-knuckled this time, until the cuts from his recent fight with Reeves start to open up on his face. "What are you tryin' to prove?" Joey asks, "What does it prove?" Like a sibling might in the playground, Jake tweaks his brother's cheek, as radio big-band music wafts in through the window.

## Sparring

Jake and Joey are sparring in the ring at Gleason's Boxing Club, Joey on the receiving end of most of the punches. Salvy and two cronies Patsy and Guido are watching, apparently invited by Joey. When they leave (after saying the two sparring brothers "look like two fags up there") Jake angrily turns on his brother for arranging the visit, saying he wants nothing to do with the Mob who are only there to take his money.

## Vickie

Jake is at the open-air swimming pool when he spies a beautiful fifteen-year-old blonde. She's Vickie (Cathy Moriarty), a local girl who hangs out with Salvy and his wiseguy friends. Sitting at the poolside in a one-piece bathing suit, she looks completely desirable to Jake, who quizzes Joey as to who she is. When it transpires his brother has been out with her, Jake's grilling turns to whether Joey actually slept with this object of his lust.

"Did you bang her?"

"No."

"Tell me the truth."

"I just told you the truth. I tell you the truth the first time. You don't have to ask me again. I never do that. I always tell you the truth."

For a moment he sounds more interested in Joey's track record with her than in the girl herself, before his attention—and jealousy—turns to Salvy and the boys' relationship with her.

As Jake smolders with resentment, muttering about how he could handle these "tough guys," Vickie gets up and moves to the edge of the pool, dangling her feet in the water as the sunlight plays on her skin. Jake's clearly obsessed with her, and Joey reminds him that he's a married man—"leave the young girls for me"—while a slow-motion shot of Vickie's legs remind us once more what's on Jake's mind.

**Getting ready**
The brothers La Motta are getting ready for a Saturday night out, preening themselves in front of the mirror while Irma screams at them for acting like a pair of "faggots". "You're always hangin' out together. Why don't you fuckin' stop?" She continues shouting insults out of the window when they hit the street, clearly as jealous of their natural bonding together as of any possible sexual aspect to their relationship.

**The dance**
Jake and Joey arrive at The Annual Summer Dance, sponsored by St. Clare's Church, and sit at a table at the back with their

friend Beansey. While Jake's gaze is scouring the room for a sight of Vickie, a Catholic priest—in one of many religious references through the film—is asked to bless the table. At last Jake sets eyes on Vickie again. She's with a group of women, but soon joined by Salvy and his cohorts, the party leaving almost immediately, Vickie escorted by Salvy. The smitten Jake follows them out, pushing his way through some entrance-door trouble (it seems violence is never far from the surface) only to see the group drawing away in a smart black convertible.

### The meeting

The next day, Jake, sitting in his own fancy car—he's clearly starting to make some money out of boxing—waits as Joey asks Vickie (talking through the pool's chain-link fence) if she'd like to meet his brother. Jake comes over and is introduced, Joey adding "He's gonna be the next champ." Jake and Vickie exchange niceties through the wire mesh (in contrast to the lack of any barrier between Jake and his brother). Jake displays an unexpected (and little seen) sensitivity as he touches her fingers and responds to her comment "Nice car" with a nervous "You wanna go for a ride?", sounding more like a first-date highschool kid than the future Bronx Bull.

### First date

They're facing the camera through the car's windshield as Vickie moves closer to Jake and he puts his arms behind her, across the top of the passenger seat. In the next shot (the camera at a low angle with the two of them in the midground), a white church in the foreground seems almost lifesize for a moment until we realize they're playing miniature novelty golf. They manage to lose the ball that Vickie putts under the church, prompting a cryptic exchange if we see the church representing their future marriage: "What does that mean?" "It means the game is over."

## First love

Jake takes Vickie back to his father's apartment, where no-one is at home—"They must have gone shopping." Initially they sit facing each other at either end of a kitchen table, before Jake gets her to sit on the center chair, then on his lap. He shows her round the apartment, explaining he's bought his father the whole building, before they end up in the bedroom, both sitting stiffly upright on the edge of the bed.

When he puts his arm lightly around her waist, Vickie gets up and moves over to look at a picture on a dressing table. It's Jake and Joey in a corny boxing stance, fists poised for action. With a string of rosary beads hanging from it, the picture literally comes between them as Jake moves close to Vickie, telling her she looks beautiful. Only when he gently kisses her and strokes her cheek does the photograph, in its oval cameo mount, disappear from view. Then they move back to the bed, and we're left with the two brothers center-stage again, as a crackly phonograph record of an Italian tenor drowns out any sound of their love-making.

## Sugar Ray

A title tells us it's *La Motta vs. Sugar Ray Robinson Detroit 1943*, and the camera swings in low, rising as if we're sitting ringside, up from the fighters boots to a full view of the battle. It's La Motta's second bout with the great Sugar Ray, played by Johnny Barnes, and the one in which he defeats the champ on points after a grueling ten rounds. As Jake gains the ascendancy in the eighth, the camera moves around the elongated-looking ring like a circling bird before, like Jake, moving in for the kill. When he knocks the "invincible" Robinson out of the ropes, for a second things look speeded-up, then as La Motta steps back to await his foe's return to the ring it's suddenly slow-motion, the camera (again like Jake) being able to pause a little. La Motta is pronounced the winner in the tenth round.

**Sex**
In the foreground, Jake's feet hang over the end of the bed as Vickie stands seductively in her negligee in the half-open doorway. She asks whether they should be doing this—"You said never to touch ya before a fight"—before proceeding to the bed where Jake asks her to kiss the cuts on his face. As they start to undress she reminds him again she's not supposed to excite him before a fight, nevertheless kissing down his bruised body as she does so. Thinking better of it, Jake suddenly stops her, saying he has to fight Robinson again, he can't fool around. Pulling his shorts back on he moves to the bathroom where he pours icy water over his erection signaling that he's willing to forego sexual passion in favor of his ambition in the ring. Then Vickie appears behind him, kissing him sensually before returning to the bedroom, her legs hanging over the end of the bed as Jake's had at the beginning of the scene.

## Defeat

It's *La Motta vs. Robinson Detroit 1943*, in the Olympia Stadium. Jake's fighting Sugar Ray for the third time, and this sequence feels noticeably closer to the action; the ring looks smaller, the close-ups of the boxers are more intimate. Robinson goes down in the seventh, the press cameras flashing right in his face as he picks himself up in slow motion. But the final decision is in his favor, accompanied by jeering from the crowd and a look of disgust on the part of Jake and Joey.

## Resignation

In the stadium dressing room, Joey hurls a chair at the wall in anger at the fight's outcome. Jake looks more resigned to what might be his inevitable fate. While Joey blames the judges' decision on the fact that Sugar Ray's going into the army, Jake asks whether this is perhaps what he's "got coming" for the "bad things" he's done—redemption for past sins, through physical punishment and ultimately defeat. After asking his brother to take home Vickie, who we learn is waiting outside, Jake's alone in front of the dressing room mirror (reminiscent of the film's opening scene), looking intently at himself while the camera pans down to a close-up of his swollen hand soaking in a bucket of ice-filled water.

## Home movies

A series of grainy amateur-looking home movies, shot in color, are intercut with various still photographs, step-motion shots, and freeze-frame images from La Motta's next six victories in the ring from 1944 to 1947. First we get three stills (*La Motta vs. Zivic Detroit January 14, 1944*) of Jake brutally downing his foe, which are followed by home footage of Jake, Vickie, and Joey, leaning against Jake's flashy convertible. Then a two-photo montage from *La Motta vs. Basora New York August 10, 1945* prefaces Jake and Vickie's civil wedding ceremony, while step-motion and freeze frames of *La Motta vs. Kochan New York September 17, 1945* are followed by more jerky family footage.

This time Vickie is the center of attention as she and Jake fool by the swimming pool and in the water, then she opens a gift from Jake of a white turban. Donning sunglasses, her "Lana Turner" look is complete. Two more black-and-white stills (*La Motta vs. Edgar Detroit June 12, 1946*) take us into Joey's rooftop reception (they couldn't afford to hire a hall) after his marriage to Lenore—confetti, cake, all the family, a regular wedding party.

The briefest of freeze frames credited as *La Motta vs. Satterfield Chicago September 12, 1946* take us into the final home footage, with Jake carrying Vickie "over the threshold" to their new home, and Vickie, Lenore, and Joey playing with their children while Jake organizes the barbeque. The whole section ends with *La Motta vs. Bell New York March 14, 1947*, a sequence of five stills showing Jake in victory mode yet again.

## Suspicion

*Pelham Parkway Bronx, New York 1947* introduces a scene in the kitchen of the La Motta home. Jake is in shorts and vest, starting to look a little heavier than previously, talking to Joey. Lenore is by her husband's side with their baby, Vickie is in the background busy at the sink. Jake's admonishing his manager-brother for making a deal so he can fight a new boy Tony Janiro, which will entail him losing thirteen pounds of weight. Joey reasons that if Jake beats the up-and-coming Janiro he's on his way to a title contest, if he loses then at least all the fighters who won't fight Jake because they're scared will change their minds— likewise the path to a title challenge. Joey tells Jake, "If you win, you win. If you lose, you still win. There's no way you can lose," adding "Just get down to 155 pounds, you fat bastard. You stop eatin'."

Vickie, who like Joey's wife doesn't take part in any of this conversation (except to respond to Jake's incessant demand for coffee) suddenly comments: "Joey's right, he [Janiro] is an up-an-coming fighter, he's good lookin', he's popular ..." This immediately sets Jake off—"Whatd'ya mean, good lookin'?"—the start of a spiral of suspicion and jealousy that will eventually drive her from him. When Jake orders her out of the room with the baby, Lenore comments that Vickie "didn't mean nothin'," at which Joey turns on his wife "Who asked you?", ordering her out of the kitchen, too.

Once both women are out of the way, the brothers cease their arguing and close ranks, with Joey suggesting that Jake goes to a training camp—"No distractions, no wives, no phone calls, nobody to bother you around." Jake replies that, while he's away, he wants his brother to keep an eye on his wife. Once again he questions how Vickie would know that Janiro is good looking, to which Joey responds "You make him ugly, what's the difference?" He suggests Jake makes it up with Vickie before he goes to training camp, "Go inside, be nice to her, make up with her ..." Jake goes into the room where the two women are sitting with their children, awkwardly putting his arms round his wife and kissing her, eventually stretched out on the floor, while his sister-in-law plays with the babies.

## Copacabana

A painted sign tells us we're at the famed Copacabana night club, then a sweeping long shot over the audience is accompanied by the voice of a comedian welcoming Jake La Motta as "the world's leading middleweight contender, the Bronx bull, the raging bull."

He's with Vickie and Joey, who has a girlfriend with him. Vickie makes her way to the bathroom, and is met on the way by Salvy who greets her with a polite kiss, saying he's with the old crowd if she can make it over for a drink. We see Salvy from Jake's viewpoint, in slow motion, as he comes over to say hello, limply shaking Jake's hand. As Salvy asks Joey to come over and have a drink with the boss, Tommy Como, Jake's attention turns to their table, coldly studying them before spitting after the departing Salvy.

On her way back from the bathroom, Vickie stops by Tommy Como's table to briefly say hello. We hear someone refer to Jake as "that fuckin' gorilla" as she returns to her table, where Jake, incensed, starts interrogating her about being interested in other men. Just then the building tension is interrupted by a round of drinks arriving, sent over by Tommy Como. Joey goes to say hello to Como, who then gestures to Jake to come over. Jake reluctantly makes his way over, where Tommy greets him patronizingly while asking him about the Janiro fight. As Jake gets carried away with what he's going to do to Janiro, he gets into some confused

e Niro as La Motta. Although the film was in black and white, the studio produced some  publicity shots in color

*The real Jake La Motta, with his second wife Vickie and their first child, Jackie, New York 1947*

obert De Niro sits with Jake La Motta at a New York boxing match in 1980, the year of the film's release

*Cathy Moriarty, the young unknown who was cast as Jake La Motta's long-suffering wife Vickie, here in the role that made her famous*

*When he was picked for the part of Joey La Motta, the movie was a similar stepping stone to success for actor Joe Pesci*

*Another color still, an overweight De Niro as the corpulent Jake La Motta going through his nightclub routine*

Moriarty and De Niro in the scene by the pool, where Jake tells the men from the press he's retiring from boxing

*Martin Scorsese in the ring, directing Robert De Niro in one of the movie's highly choreographed fight sequences*

*Knock out: De Niro's La Motta downs an opponent, surrounded by baying fans and omnipresent photographers*

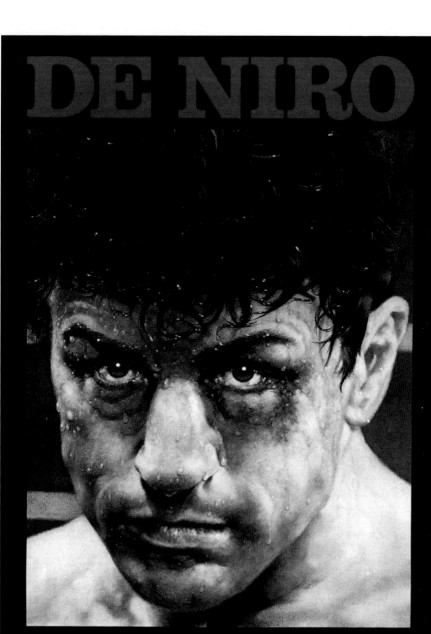

*A movie icon: posters and publicity photos for Raging Bull became collector's items as the film achieved cult status*

sado-sexual banter with Salvy. "He's a pretty kid, too. I mean I don't know, I gotta problem if I should fuck him or fight him." Clearly his suspicions about his wife are but one part of more fundamental psychological hang-ups.

## Obsession

Later that night. Vickie is asleep in bed as Jake enters the room in the dark, prowling round the bed and back, checking if she's asleep before sitting down. He wakes her, asking her whether she ever thinks of other men when they make love. Once again he mentions Janiro, but this time it's with anxiety rather than anger in his voice. He's becoming obsessed, haunted by his own fears of losing her to other men.

## Janiro

Suddenly cutting to the fourth fight scene, we have an image of Janiro's face being pummeled even before the title *La Motta vs. Janiro New York 1947* appears on the screen. Jake's assault is merciless, and the camera's close-up depiction of it graphic, as blood spurts from his opponent's open wounds, Janiro's nose crunching under the blows. When he hits the canvas, virtually unconscious, we see what "knock out" really means. Near the ringside Tommy Como is heard commenting, "He ain't pretty no more." As the victorious Jake swaggers around the ring in triumph, Vickie realizes he has demonstrated more than just the desire to win—he really is becoming a raging bull, driven by jealousy and anger. As if to emphasize his increasing isolation, the scene shifts briefly to Jake barely visible in the steam room, working out to lose more weight, as his trainer insists "four pounds."

## Copacabana 2

Another shot of the crowd at the Copacabana prefaces Joey talking at the bar about Jake's prospects as a title contender now that he's beaten Janiro. His eyes are distracted, though he carries on conversing, as he sees Vickie coming in with Salvy and company.

He goes over to their table, and takes his sister-in-law into the hat-check area where he asks her what she's playing at; Vickie replying that she feels she's a prisoner—"I'm tired of havin' to turn around and havin' both of yuz up my ass all the time"—in a situation where the man she loves (telling Joey that she *does* love Jake) no longer even has sex with her. Joey assures her all will be fine once Jake has a shot at the title:

"… then everything will be OK …

"Jake's never gonna be champ. Too many people hate him."

"And you're drinkin' with them."

Joey follows her over to Salvy's table, telling her, "You're makin' an asshole out of my brother," as Salvy insists there's nothing going on. Joey appears to calm down for a second as Vickie starts to make her exit, leaning over in a conciliatory way to Salvy before exploding in anger and smashing a glass in his face. Here we see the ugly similarity between Joey and Jake, with anger triggering out-of-control violence as the brawl spills out onto the street. Joey attacks Salvy over the head with one of the metal stands supporting the velvet rope across the club entrance, kicks him while he's on the ground then continuously slams a cab door into Salvy's body.

## Reconciliation

A shot of the doorway, a close-up of the window signage, and a shot of the licence certificate hanging on the wall tells us we're at the Debonair Social Club (members only). It's daytime—there's coffee brewing and clean cups ready —and Tommy Como has convened a peace-making between Joey and Salvy. The two shake hands, then when Salvy—his arm in a sling after the previous night's violence —leaves, Tommy persuades Joey that Jake's only chance of making it is with the Mob on his side. "He thinks he's gonna walk in there and become champion on his own. Huh? ... he's got no respect for nobody." Tommy makes it plain to Joey what he has to do: "You're a smart kid, you go to him, you tell him ..."

## Choices

People are scattering out of the rain as Joey runs through the entrance to the open-air public swimming pool, where he's meeting Jake. It's where his brother and Vickie met, as Jake reminds him as he goes on to continue his obsessive concern about his wife's supposed infidelity. Joey, not revealing that he'd seen Vickie in Salvy's company, tells his brother he's got two options: "Throw her out ... either that or live with her and let her ruin your life, 'cause that's what's happenin'."

They go on to discuss what came of Joey's meeting with Como. Joey tells Jake it's the old "good news, bad news routine." The good news is he'll get a shot at the title, the bad news being that he'll have to throw a fight—"do the old flip-flop for 'em." Jake now seems reconciled to the idea of cooperating with the Mob, and at their price: "So what else is new?..."

"What you expect, you know that was coming?"

"Eh, you win some, you lose some ..."

"This one you lose."

## Bets off

Jake's next opponent, Billy Fox, is on the scales at the pre-match weigh-in, then it's Jake's turn. Their weights are ceremoniously announced to awaiting pressmen by the an official of the boxing commission, a worried-looking Jackie Curtie (played by La Motta biographer Peter Savage). Then suddenly the camera is moving down the cavernous corridors in the basement, where Curtie is telling Jake and Joey how he's worried about rumors that the fight is being fixed. There are suspicions as to why, after being favorite, Jake is suddenly the "twelve-to-five underdog." As Jake insists he's never thrown a fight, and never intends to, Curtie tells them that "bets are off on this one."

## The dive

A ringside bell heralds Madison Square Garden, it's *La Motta vs. Fox New York 1947*. As the ring announcer introduces the fighters, the camera concentrates on interested parties in the crowd—Curtie, Salvy, Tommy Como— prior to the fight commencing. Jake's first punches start to give things away, as he knocks Fox into the ropes then feigns punches to his opponent's head and body. The crowd get increasingly agitated as Jake takes more punches unnecessarily, letting Fox overwhelm him, but he's too proud to literally "take a dive." This makes the outcome look even more obviously fixed, and the camera follows a despondent Jake out of the ring amid booing spectators, as Billy Fox is announced the winner on a technical knock-out. In his dressing room, Jake weeps in the arms of his trainer—"What'd I do?"—as press men try in vain to get to him.

## Suspension

The next day the *New York Daily News* headline announces "BOARD SUSPENDS LA MOTTA". The purse for the bout has been withheld pending a district attorney's probe, because it seemed obvious that Jake took a dive. Throwing the newspaper on the kitchen table, Jake protests to Joey that he's thrown the match, what more do they want? Joey insists his brother should have been more convincing in his defeat, going down for instance. Jake's pride wouldn't allow that: "You don't understand, I had to fight a bum, he was a bum." Now he feels that he looks like a bum himself.

The two brothers sit either side of a table in a diner, eating chicken wings, Joey telling him not to worry, he'll get his title shot now, Tommy Como won't forget him.

## Waiting

*Two Years Later, Detroit June 15, 1949* and it's raining outside the Book-Cadillac hotel, where (a welcome board in the lobby tells us) Jake La Motta is staying prior to his title fight with the middleweight champion, the Frenchman Marcel Cerdan. Jake's pacing up and down in his room, irritable because the fight, at the open-air Biggs Stadium, been postponed for twenty-four hours on account of the weather. His trainers and assistants are there, practicing how quickly they can stitch up a wound ringside, as are Vickie and Joey. Joey suggests they order some food from room service, and when Vickie says she'll just have cake, he suggests she might prefer a cheeseburger. Right away, this "interest" in his wife raises Jake's suspicions about Vickie, this time in his brother's direction.

As Jake lies down in the bedroom, alone with his thoughts, a knock comes on the door. It's Tommy Como, calling by to wish him luck. After a brief conversation, Tommy's about to leave and Vickie kisses him goodbye. Jake watches as Tommy kisses her again, his hands around her face, telling her how beautiful she is, Joey appearing to tacitly agree as he too gazes at her. It's a slow-motion moment that we can see burning itself on Jake's mind.

As soon as Tommy leaves Jake confronts Vickie for being "so friendly" with the mobster. They're framed in a narrow doorway, Joey watching from the foreground of the picture. To the left, a mirror reflects the trainers, apparently oblivious to what's going on. As Jake slaps Vickie for having "disrespect," Joey tells him to stop it. Jake turns on his brother, telling him to shut up—"I'll fuckin' take care of you later"— before going back to the bedroom, slamming the door behind him.

### The moment

An abrupt cut to Jake punching Joey, who's holding a rubber mat to his body as part of some pre-match sparring. Jake stops and begins making his way out of the room, Joey adjusting the hood on his robe as he walks in front of his entourage. It's the beginning of the long steady-cam tracking shot that takes us up through the subterranean environs of the stadium then down through the roaring crowd to the ring, where Jake will meet the champion in his challenge for the title.

## Triumph

The boxing gloves of the two fighters "shaking hands" are shown in freeze-frame under *La Motta vs. Middleweight Champion Marcel Cerdan Detroit 1949*. This prefaces a spectacularly edited sequence in which Jake gets the better of his opponent with increasingly punishing ferocity. By the beginning of the tenth round, the title-holder can take no more, and La Motta is pronounced the new champ on a technical knock-out. In contrast with the fast-cut editing of the actual fight, Jake's moment of triumph as he raises his arms in victory is shown in more contemplative slow-motion. And as real time resumes with him donning the middleweight belt, a rarely seen look of peaceful satisfaction passes across his face.

## Paranoia

The noise of the flashbulbs exploding around the ring segues into the sound of Jake shaking a faulty television, trying to get it to work. The title tells us it's *Pelham Parkway New York 1950* and he's in his living room with Joey, who tells him not to shake the set like that—"It's the worst thing you can do." Jake's looking heavier, and we can see he's halfway through a hero sandwich. Vickie comes in from shopping, kissing Joey then Jake, and when she goes upstairs Jake asks his brother what the idea is, kissing his wife on the mouth. Joey lets it pass, then mentions that he can't see what's happening with the television because Jake's stomach is obscuring the screen. He gets another dirty look from his brother, but goes on—"You're supposed to be the champion, but you're eatin' like there's no tomorrow," reminding him he has a title fight the next month—as Jake takes a swig from a bottle of beer.

Tension mounts as Jake starts harking back two years to the night when Joey fought with Salvy at the Copa. When Joey insists it had nothing to do with Vickie, Jake won't accept it, in a confrontation that's pivotal to the whole film:

"Joey, don't lie to me."

"I'm not lying."

"What do I look like to you, huh?"

"Hey, I'm your brother. You're supposed to believe me. Don't you trust me?"

"No I don't."

"Oh you don't? That's nice."

"I don't trust you when it comes to her. I don't trust nobody ..."

Suddenly the paranoia that's been building up in Jake throughout the movie comes to a head as he twists and turns the conversation, first suggesting that Salvy was having an affair with Vickie, then Tommy Como, then accusing his own brother:

"You fucked my wife?"

"What?!"

"You fucked my wife?"

Joey is incredulous:

"How could you ask me a question like that? How could you ask me? I'm your brother. You ask me that?"

Jake persists in the question, which Joey refuses to answer, telling his brother he's cracking up: "You know what you should do? Try a little more fuckin' and a little less eatin'. You won't have troubles upstairs in your bedroom, and you won't take it out on me and everybody else." As Joey leaves, Jake stands immobile in the middle of the room for a moment, then with a slow sense of purpose walks into the hallway and up the stairs.

## Trauma

Vickie is making the bed as Jake enters the room. He walks round, and starts stroking her hair as he asks her where she's been that day. She tells him she's been to the movies with her sister, after which his hand tightens on her hair as he starts asking about the night at the Copacabana. His line of questioning takes the same paranoid route as with Joey a few minutes before—but more directly, as he pulls her hair, slaps her across the face, and asks "Did you fuck my brother?"

After he hits her again and throws her on the bed, Vickie rushes out of the room and into the bathroom, where she locks herself in. Jake escalates his questioning, now asking her *why*, not *if*, she slept with Joey. She tells him he's sick and refuses to open the door, at which point he bursts in, the door crashing to the floor. Jake walks towards the camera, which pans round as he traps Vickie in the corner, shaking her by the hair and demanding to know why she did it.

Vickie momentarily turns the emotional tables on him by "confessing" to his charges and more—confirming what he's asking to hear, and knowing it's not what he *wants* to hear. She's punishing him and at the same time giving him an emotional way out of his frustrations. "I fucked all of them! What do you want me to say? ... I fucked all of them—Tommy, Salvy, your brother! All of them!" Jake slaps her round the face again as she continues with a catalogue of sexual taunting. He's about to punch her, his fist raised, when he changes his mind, pushing her away and rushing out of the house.

As Jake strides down the sidewalk towards his brother's house, Vickie is right behind, pulling him and screaming. He knocks her to the ground, and delivers several blows which are obscured from the camera's view by a parked car. Joey and his family are eating dinner, Joey threatening to "stab" his small son if he doesn't keep his fingers out of his plate. In the background, Jake appears through the front door, striding towards the dinner table. He lunges at his brother, dragging him off his chair, screaming that he's been "fuckin' my wife" while beating and kicking him viciously in front of his family. As the two wives drag him off, Jake delivers the punch he held back in the bathroom, knocking Vickie out. He leaves the house, where the final shot is of Joey's two children looking traumatized.

**Embrace**

His television is still without a picture, and Jake sits in the dark staring at it. In the background we see Vickie coming in, going straight upstairs. In the bedroom she starts packing things to leave, and Jake comes in. He follows her round the room as she gets clothes out of drawers, touching her tentatively and begging forgiveness—"I'm a bum without you and the kids. Don't go." As he puts an arm on her shoulder she turns to him, looking him up and down, then accepts his embrace, burying her head in his shoulder.

**Defender**

The image abruptly jump-cuts into *La Motta vs. Dauthuille Detroit 1950* with a shot of Jake receiving a punch to the face. He's defending his title against another Frenchman, and taking a lot of punishment. Then, in one of the most tensely choreographed fight sequences in the movie, we see Jake make an amazing comeback, as in the final seconds he turns on his opponent with a frenzy of punches to the body and jaw. The announcer yells "he's been playing possum" as La Motta batters his challenger to the canvas, retaining the championship.

## Phone call

After the fight, Jake walks with Vickie along a corridor in the arena. She's urging him to make things up with Joey, just to make a phone call and say he's sorry—"He's your brother. You have to talk to him sooner or later." Jake relents, giving his wife the change to actually dial the number. While she's in the phone booth Jake is approached by a reporter—Jake starts to get agitated with the newsman because he won't go away, then Vickie motions him she's got through. He takes the phone but remains silent, closing the booth door and just listening as Joey answers "Hello. Hello?" Joey thinks it's Salvy or some other joker—"I know somebody's there. I can hear you breathin' "—and hurls obscenities down the phone. Jake, looking emotionless, with his battered and bruised face half in shadow, hangs up.

## Bloodbath

The first image of Jake La Motta's fifth confrontation with his old adversary Sugar Ray Robinson is of his back being sponged down with bloody water from the corner bucket. As he lies back, already looking defeated, his trainer passes his hands over him, almost in a rite of religious blessing as he administers the mouthshield like the sacrament at holy communion. A television announcement for Pabst beer tells us it's "the fight of the year" as Jake appears more and more the loser, while Joey and his wife are watching the fight at home.

The thirteenth round sees Robinson inflicting the kind of damage on La Motta that the latter usually hands out. As Sugar Ray pauses between punches (perhaps waiting for his opponent to go down) Jake yells to him "Come on, come on", refusing to give up, though leaning back on the ropes for support, "C'mon Ray." The image of Robinson slows to almost a standstill as he comes towards the defiant Jake, from whose perspective we see the first of a torrent of murderous punches.

Blood spurts from Jake's face, from his nose, from his eyes, and we see Vickie in the crowd, burying her face in her hands. Blood runs down Jake's body and legs amid the sounds of muffled animal roars, screams from the crowd, and the explosion of flashbulbs. Then, after a sudden silence as Robinson closes in for the kill, a last series of blows sends Jake's blood spattering onto the ringside spectators as the fight is stopped. We see Vickie covering her face again, Joey looking dazed in front of his television, while Jake lurches over to Sugar Ray's corner—"Hey, Ray, I never went down, man! You never got me down, Ray ..." The announcer climbs into the ring to declare Robinson the new champion after a technical knock-out, as the camera pans to a close-up of Jake's blood dripping off the ropes, an image Scorsese first witnessed at a real-life fight in Madison Square Garden.

## Florida

Under the title card *Miami 1956* we see cars in the driveway of Jake's Florida home. He's by the poolside with his wife and three children, talking to reporters about his pulling out of an imminent match.

"Why are you pulling out of Wednesday's fight Jake ?"

Looking older and heavier—he's put on about fifty pounds in weight—he tells the pressmen he's retired from boxing.

"It's over for me. Boxing's over for me."

He goes on to talk about having to worry about "the weight" all the time, how he's through with it even though boxing's been good to him—he's got a nice house, great kids, a beautiful wife. Cigar in mouth, he gets the photographer to take some shots of the whole family, as he talks about the nightclub he's just opened. "Guess what I'm gonna call it ? Take a guess."

## Stand-up

A roll of drums brings us to "Jake La Motta's," the club he's opened on Collins Avenue. Jake sits at the bar as the band plays an intro to his stand-up comedy routine. The jokes aren't funny, the sexual references are crude, the crowd's response sycophantic; Jake shows little respect for the audience, but at least can laugh at himself—"I haven't seen so many losers since my last fight at Madison Square Garden."

Offstage, he's introduced to a local state attorney and his wife, and in the space of seconds makes an unfunny remark about the attorney taking back-handers, spills a drink over his wife, and jokes about his own wife Vickie not coming to the club to "let you bums get involved with her." Two girls who can't get served at the bar because they look under-age tell Jake their problem. He lets one kiss him—"Any girl who can kiss like that can drink in my joint any time"— then the other, to "prove" they are both twenty-one. A doo-wop record plays in the background—The Hearts with "Lonely Nights," pleading "I miss you so much, please come home"— as Jake pours champagne into a "tower" of five glasses, disregarding a member of staff who tells him his wife's outside.

### Leaving

Jake trudges outside to where Vickie is waiting in the driving seat of their Cadillac. It's dawn. She tells him from behind the partly opened window (the artificial barrier reminiscent of the fence they spoke through when they first met) that's she leaving him. He asks her to open the door and to move over, but she refuses—"What, so you can put your hands on me?"—before telling him she's seen a lawyer and everything's set up. "I already made up my mind. I'm leavin'. That's it. The kids are gonna be with me. And if you show your face around, I'm gonna call the cops on you, all right?" She pulls away, leaving a cloud of dust wafting over Jake, a sad figure standing alone in the car park before he makes his way back to the club.

### Arrest

Now apart from Vickie, Jake lies asleep, alone, when he's woken by two deputies from the DA's office. They show him the picture of a schoolgirl and what appears to be a much older young woman. Both pictures are of one of the girls he allowed as a "twenty-one-year-old" into his club. It transpired the girls were prostitutes, using the club to solicit custom. Jake is arrested for "introducing" the under-age girls to men.

## Bail

Out on bail, Jake calls on Vickie to just "pick up one thing." It's his championship belt, and he needs $10,000 to pay off the cops and get the case dropped. The belt is standing displayed against the picture of Jake and Joey that we saw when he and Vickie first made love. He forces the jewels out of the belt as Vickie asks why can't he get the money from his friends. "What friends?" he replies.

He tries to sell the jewels, but is only offered $1500—the jeweler says he could have got a good price for the whole belt.

## Solitary

*Dade County Stockade Florida 1957*: Jake is being man-handled and bundled into the darkness of a barren cell, struggling and fighting all the way as he has through his life. But now he's truly alone with his demons, there's no-one else there to take his anger out on. It's a time for redemption through self-punishment as he bangs his head, his fists, and arms against the hard cell wall, screaming "Why, why, why'd you do it?" then breaking down in tears. "I'm not an animal. Why do you treat me like this? I'm not so bad …"—desperate pleas addressed to himself as much as the world out there, a world that has turned its back on its former champion.

## Reunion

Now out of jail, Jake's up on stage again (*New York City 1958*) this time in the seedy bar— the Carnevale Lounge— of the Hotel Markwell. He's telling his usual near-the-knuckle jokes, exchanging insults with customers drinking at the long bar, and introducing a stripper ("Emma 48s") who struts her stuff in time-honored burlesque fashion.

As Jake emerges from the club, hailing a cab for him and his stripper girlfriend, he spots the familiar figure of Joey going into an all-night deli across the road. Saying he'll "be home later," he puts Emma into the cab and approaches Joey as he leaves the shop. His brother ignores him, walking down the street as Jake calls after him. He catches up with him in an indoor car park, the moustached Joey looking older now. No longer the old aggressive Jake, he begs his brother to "forgive and forget," Joey seeming initially embarrassed by what to him is an uncharacteristic show of affection. Jake persists, as he had in previous reconciliations with Vickie, putting his arm around Joey's shoulder, hugging him and kissing him. Joey unwinds a little, as he climbs in his car promising to call Jake in a couple of days.

### Finale

The billboard outside the Barbizon Plaza Theatre announces "An Evening with Jake La Motta"—we're back at the 1964 start of the film, but this time we get to read the full blurb, which continues: "featuring the works of Paddy Chayefsky, Rod Serling, Shakespeare, Budd Schulberg, Tennessee Williams. Tonight 8:30."

In his far-from-salubrious dressing room, an even more corpulent Jake is going through his act as before, one of its features being the famous back-of-a-cab scene with Marlon

Brando talking to his "brother" Rod Steiger in *On The Waterfront*. Jake introduces it as being about "an up-and-comer who's now a down-and-outer"—a parallel of his own life, as is much of the Budd Schulberg script itself. "You remember that night at the Garden you came down in my dressing room and you said, 'Kid, this ain't your night; we're going for the price on Wilson?' Remember that? 'This ain't your night?' My night. I could've taken Wilson apart that night."

"You was my brother. You should've looked out for me a little bit. You should've looked out for me just a little bit. You should've taken care of me just a little bit instead o' making me take them dives for the short-end money."

Such lines resonate strongly in the context of Jake's life, no more so than the now-iconic speech: "You don't understand. I coulda had class. I coulda been a contender. I coulda been somebody instead of a bum, which is what I am." The significance of the *Waterfront* speech in terms of Jake's own relationship with his brother is obvious, but the wider implications are more profound. As he runs through the monologue in the mirror, we know he's addressing his audience, telling them how he feels, but also himself. When he says "It was *you* Charley," he's talking not about his own brother Joey, but directly to the reflection in the mirror—he seems to be admitting to himself, at last, that he's been his own worst enemy.

A stagehand (played by Martin Scorsese) appears, telling La Motta he's got five minutes. Adjusting his bow tie, cigar in mouth, Jake prepares himself once more for the arena—"Go get 'em, champ"—as he shadow boxes out of our sight and to his public. All we are left with in the last frames of the film is the empty mirror, as we hear Jake chanting to himself, "I'm the boss, I'm the boss, I'm the boss, I'm the boss, I'm the boss …"

## Epilogue

The final titles carry a biblical quotation, signifying Jake La Motta's final redemption, brought about through seeing himself clearly for the first time:

*So, for the second time, [the Pharisees]*
*summoned the man who had been blind and said:*
*"Speak the truth before God.*
*We know this fellow is a sinner."*
*"Whether or not he is a sinner, I do not know,"*
*the man replied.*
*"All I know is this:*
*once I was blind and now I can see."*

The quote, which appears one or two lines at a time, is followed by a dedication:

*Remembering Haig P. Manoogian, teacher.*
*May 23, 1916—May 26, 1980.*
*With love and resolution, Marty.*

Haig Manoogian was Martin Scorsese's great mentor, his professor when he studied film at New York University. He died of a heart attack just before *Raging Bull* was completed.

# the decision

## Public and critical reaction

The reluctance with which the studio had approached *Raging Bull* in the first place was repeated when they saw the final cut. It was clear to them that this wasn't a commercial movie, in the sense that it was going to be an automatic box office success, or even that there were many angles with which to sell it to mass audiences.

Scorsese had shown the film to Andy Albeck, David Bach, and other studio executives in the middle of July 1980 at the MGM screening room on 55th Street in New York. Bach describes the scene in Peter Biskind's *Easy Riders, Raging Bulls*: "The lights came up slowly in a room full of silence, as if the viewers had lost all powers of speech. Nor was there the customary applause. Martin Scorsese leaned against the back wall of the screening room as if cowering from the silence. Then Andy Albeck rose from his seat, marched briskly to him, shook his hand just once, and said quietly 'Mr. Scorsese, you are an Artist.'" Biskind goes on to tell how, after the screening, Scorsese had asked a young woman what she thought about the movie; her anguished reaction was to break into tears and run down the hall. From there on in, as Biskind puts it, he knew he was not making a "likeable" movie.

During the long post-production period, according to Irwin Winkler, United Artists had even tried to quietly sell it off to another company, but were unable to find any takers.

Now they had the finished product on their hands, they didn't seem to know quite what to do with it, so almost released it by default while they concentrated their marketing strategy on Michael Cimino's $36 million *Heaven's Gate*. (To no avail, of course. The over-budget and, as they saw it, overlong Western epic was drastically cut, consequently panned by the critics, and a disaster at the box office. Only when a "director's cut" was released years later, with the deleted scenes restored, did the movie get a favorable critical response).

### The press

*Raging Bull* opened at the Sutton, Cinerama 1 and other theaters in New York on November 14 1980, and was greeted with enthusiasm by some of the critics. In *Newsweek* Jack Kroll felt it was "the best movie of the year," while Vincent Canby gave it an absolute rave review in the *New York Times*.

Stating in his opening salvo that Scorsese "has made his most ambitious film as well as his finest," Canby went on to describe the film as being "humane in the way of unsentimental fiction that understands that a life—any life—can only be appreciated when the darkness that surrounds it is acknowledged." Referring to the scene in the jail stockade where Jake whimpers "I'm not an animal," he acknowledges the essential humanity that is central to the film: "Though there's not one sequence in the film when he hasn't behaved like an animal, Jake, like all the rest of us, is the kind of animal who can ask a question."

Lavishing particular praise on Cathy Moriarty's performance ("Either she is one of the film finds of the decade or Mr. Scorsese is Svengali. Perhaps both"), the review was one any filmmaker or actor would die for. Canby concluded his 900-word piece thus: "And at the heart of the film, there is the mystery of Jake himself, but that is what separates *Raging Bull* from all other fight movies, in fact, from most movies about anything. *Raging Bull* is an achievement."

And *Time* magazine recognized in particular De Niro's participation being at the core of the movie's dynamic when it commented, "Much of *Raging Bull* exists because of the possibilities it offers De Niro to display his own explosive art."

In Toronto, Canada, where the film opened simultaneously with New York and Los Angeles, the *Globe and Mail* writer Jay Scott—while applauding the sheer power of the movie—had one reservation. "Overall, *Raging Bull* is so tough … and so intransigently anti-romantic that some viewers are certain to wonder why it was made at all. Where's the *moral?*"

On the other side of the Atlantic, Steve Jenkins wrote in the British Film Institute's prestigious *Monthly Film Journal*: "*Raging Bull* may prove to be Scorsese's finest achievement to date. Certainly the visceral intelligence on display, the radical awareness and *use* of his own cinephilia, the creation of a fractured biography productively shot through with personal obsessions, make it a powerful contender."

## The public

Like *Mean Streets* seven years before, *Raging Bull* went down well with audiences in New York (where there seemed to be more acceptance of "art house" movies among the main-stream public), but was a difficult one to sell elsewhere. Understandably so, in that the film basically made for uncomfortable viewing. And that wasn't just true of the nineteen minutes of fight sequences, although the depiction of the savagery in the ring was unprecedented even in boxing movies.

Both the physical violence and undercurrent of anger throughout the picture was unsettling—and this, of course, was Scorsese's intent. Director Steven Spielberg spoke of the unease he experienced watching the domestic confrontations in *Raging Bull*, likening it to sneaking through your neighbors' open door and listening to them arguing, knowing full well you shouldn't really be there.

Similar to when Scorsese and others first read the La Motta autobiography that De Niro thrust upon them, reaction to the film was colored by the fact that the central character came over as a very unpleasant person. *Variety* magazine caught the mood when it described De Niro's La Motta as "one of the most repugnant and unlikeable screen protagonists in some time," feeling that the film seemed to deliberately set out to alienate its audience. It was a view mirrored almost word for word in the *New York Daily News*, Kathleen Carroll describing Jake as "one of the most repugnant characters in the history of the movies," and criticizing Scorsese for ignoring La Motta's reform school past and "offering no explanation as to his anti-social behavior." Thelma Schoonmaker would recall how "Marty and I read the first revue and it basically said 'Don't distribute this movie ... no one will come and see it.'"

With its trade-journal attention to box office potential, *Variety* headed its review "Great boxing scenes but De Niro's character a turnoff. May have wobbly legs," predicting the movie "should do well in class situations but may flounder in the mass market due to the offputting character." The showbiz bible just about got it right. Across the board, the movie—not helped by the studio's lack of promotional enthusiasm—simply bombed at the box office. It was a bitter disappointment for Martin Scorsese, after a similar fate had befallen his previous film *New York, New York*. He wanted the kind of success enjoyed by contemporaries such as George Lucas and Francis Ford Coppola (and Michael Cimino, post-*The Deer Hunter* and before the commercial disaster of *Heaven's Gate*).

Praise from the critics was fine, but without some money-makers under his belt he couldn't expect producers and studios to continue to finance his films. But he recognized that if that was the case, then so be it—*Raging Bull* could very well be his last movie. "The idea had been to make the film as openly honest as possible, with no concessions at all for box office or audience. I said 'That's it. This is the end of my career. This is the final one.'"

## Recognition

High-profile recognition did come, however, with the Oscar nominations for the 1980 Academy Awards. Producer Robert Chartoff had seen it coming: "I knew we had a great movie, but I didn't realize until I saw it in its totality what we really did have ... I remember just going up to both of them (Scorsese and De Niro) and saying congratulations, you're gonnna win the Oscar ... Of course I was half right, but it was clear that this was a very special movie." Scorsese, on the other hand, was more circumspect about its chances: "Actually I was very surprised it got some Academy Award nominations. It was the first nomination I got as Best Director."

In all, *Raging Bull* received eight nominations—for Best Picture, Best Director, Best Actor, Best Supporting Actor (Joe Pesci), Best Supporting Actress (Cathy Moriarty), Best Cinematography, Best Sound, and Best Editing.

The Oscar ceremony itself, set for March 30 1981, was postponed for the first time in its history, after the assassination attempt on President Ronald Reagan earlier that day by John Hinkley. Hinkley was a Jodie Foster obsessive, and had been stalking the star. After the Reagan shooting, connections were immediately made with *Taxi Driver* when Hinkley confessed he had modeled his role as would-be presidential assassin on that of Foster's screen savior Travis Bickle. The ceremony took place the following day, by which time the Hinkley/*Taxi Driver* story had broken, and Scorsese was shadowed at the ceremony by FBI bodyguards, who ushered him out before the Best Picture was announced, telling him "the Redford picture was going to win anyway."

In the event the relatively bland Robert Redford-directed film, *Ordinary People, did* get the Best Picture award, with *Raging Bull* winning two—De Niro for Best Actor and Thelma Schoonmaker for the editing. Newcomer Cathy Moriarty was more than delighted just to have been nominated: "It was very nice, I guess it means that I was pretty good in a certain day of my life, right? So that means a lot to me." Michael Chapman likewise was happy with a nomination for Cinematography: "I'm very proud to have been nominated, it's wonderful to be nominated. I didn't win, so I don't know if it's wonderful to win … but it's much sadder that Marty didn't win, isn't that ridiculous?"

Indeed Scorsese's, quarter-century absence from the Best Director winners' list—and his sometimes bitter view on it—started right then. "When I lost for *Raging Bull*," Scorsese would reflect "that's when I realized what my place in the system would be, if I did survive at all—on the outside looking in."

Other awards were showered on the movie. Robert De Niro won Best Actor honors from the Golden Globes, the New York Film Critics Circle, the Los Angeles Film Critics Association, and the National Board of Review. Joe Pesci was chosen as Best Supporting Actor by the New York Film Critics Circle, the National Board of Review, and the National Society of Film Critics. The National Society of Film Critics also honored Michael Chapman with its Best Cinematography citation, while the Los Angeles Film Critics Association chose *Raging Bull* as Best Picture for 1980. It was also chosen to open the Berlin Film Festival in February 1981.

But the biggest award for those taking part was to have been involved in the first place, as Cathy Moriarty would acknowledge: "It gave me a wonderful opportunity in my life, and I got to prove something. And I got to step up to the plate. Obviously I was OK, so I thank them [De Niro and Scorsese] for that." Thelma Schoonmaker felt similarly privileged just to have been part of it—"It was such an amazing experience to be thrust into something that powerful, and in an environment I didn't know and was ill at ease in, then have it be so rewarding."

The film's eventual long-term recognition as a true masterpiece was confirmed when, at the end of the 1980s, it was voted in three polls as the greatest film of the decade. It was an honor that was particularly gratifying for Martin

Scorsese: "It was really very good for me, I liked it a lot, because it meant that the film was remembered ... and that I was still alive to see that."

In retrospect, the film has garnered more predictable accolades as it has come to be regarded as a contemporary classic. Reviewing a new print released in 2000, BBC reviewer Michael Thompson enthusiastically summed up the impact the film still made twenty years on: "Every swirling camera movement, every distinctive angle, has a real reason for existing in this story of world middleweight boxing champ Jake La Motta (Robert De Niro) who descends from unstoppable fighting machine to overweight goon, claiming victims both inside the ring and out. In what is essentially a rather frightening probe into the limitations of masculinity, the power of Scorsese is matched by the intensity of De Niro who delves deep into the soul of the boxer. It's one of those De Niro performances which probably took him years to get over, and for all we know a shrink got rich in the process. If all you know about *Raging Bull* is the famous fact that De Niro piled on weight for the role, then there really is a lot more to discover and enjoy. Be amazed."

And in 1989 the film was selected by the United States National Film Preservation Board for preservation in the National Film Registry of the Library of Congress, an honor only bestowed on twenty-five "culturally, historically, or aesthetically significant films" each year.

# changing lives

## The impact on the actors

The impact that *Raging Bull* would have on the career of all its participants was considerable, particularly in the case of its lead actors De Niro, Pesci, and Moriarty.

### The La Motta legacy

When *Raging Bull* was released, Robert De Niro was already riding high with his Oscar nomination for Michael Cimino's *The Deer Hunter*, and a track record that included, as well as Scorsese's seminal *Mean Streets* and *Taxi Driver*, Bertolucci's *1900* and *The Godfather Part II* with Francis Ford Coppola. But despite having been up there among the "big boys" for more than a decade, the sheer power of his performance as Jake La Motta would be seen as a benchmark, both by casting directors and audiences, for years to come.

By way of contrast, his Catholic priest in 1981's *True Confessions* was appropriately restrained, while the next outing with Scorsese was the complete opposite of the angst-ridden and anger-driven "Bronx Bull". Apart from also being an "unsympathetic" character, the pushy, over-confident comedian in *The King Of Comedy* (1983) was about as far from Jake La Motta as you could get.

De Niro was certainly not typecast (nor would he allow himself to be) as a result of the La Motta role, with parts that ranged from the romantic (*Falling In Love* with Meryl Streep in

131

1984) to the satanic (Alan Parker's 1987 *Angel Heart*), with a terrorist plumber in Terry Gilliam's wacky *Brazil* (1985) adding to the mix.

But the next few years also saw plenty of "tough" hard-edged roles that he and Scorsese had together created a precedent for in *Mean Streets*, *Taxi Driver*, and, most spectacularly, *Raging Bull*. The Italian "Spaghetti Western" director Sergio Leone saw him as a natural choice for the gangster "Noodles" Aaronson in his sprawling epic *Once Upon A Time In America* (1984), while in Roland Joffe's *The Mission* (1986) he played an eighteenth-century slave hunter. In 1987's *The Untouchables*, Brian De Palma had him back in gangland as Al Capone, and the Michael Mann thriller *Heat* (1995) saw De Niro's professional thief pitched against Al Pacino's equally tenacious cop.

Likewise, when he worked with Martin Scorsese once again, it was back in New York's "wise guy" territory as a ruthless Mob enforcer in 1990's *GoodFellas*. And, still with Scorsese, he struck an even more terrifying figure as the psychopathic ex-con Max Cady in the 1991 remake of the 1962 Robert Mitchum thriller *Cape Fear*—a character *Variety* magazine described as "a memorable nasty right up there with Travis Bickle and Jake La Motta."

The fourth time (and to date the last) that De Niro and Scorsese would collaborate after *Raging Bull* was in 1995's *Casino*. Again he played a hard-boiled mobster, this time moving into the Las Vegas gambling rackets along with his strongman sidekick, played by Joe Pesci. This was De Niro's fourth teaming with Pesci. After *Raging Bull* the two had appeared together in Scorsese's *GoodFellas*, then again in

*A Bronx Tale* in 1993. The story of a teenager in the Italian-American Bronx, torn between loyalty to his bus-driver father (De Niro) and the local Mob wise guys whom he gets involved with, *A Bronx Tale* was also De Niro's first film as director.

Robert De Niro is now recognized as one of the finest screen actors of his generation. Over the last decade his film parts have ranged from light comedy (*Meet The Parents* in 2000), through social satire in 1997's marvelous *Wag the Dog*, to sinister villains (*The Fan*, 1996) and again the archetypal tough-guy in *Ronin* (1998). And, opposite Brando in 2001's *The Score*, an ageing burglar who can't resist one last heist. Despite his consummate skill and effortlessly charismatic presence in front of the camera, the quality of De Niro's films haven't always matched up to his reputation as an actor—a reputation forged in epic performances, of which his Jake La Motta in *Raging Bull* is still regarded as his most powerful.

## Acting the hard man

Having been catapulted out of obscurity when Robert De Niro and Martin Scorsese offered him the role of Joey La Motta, the impact of *Raging Bull* on Joe Pesci's career is incalculable. After his appearance in *The Death Collector* in 1976—which first attracted the attention of De Niro when he was watching late night television—the former child actor and nightclub entertainer had given up on movies as a job option and settled happily into running a restaurant. Just four years later, after *Raging Bull*, he'd been nominated for an Academy Award for Best Supporting Actor.

From there on in, the work came thick and fast, starting with *I'm Dancing As Fast As I Can* and *Dear Mr. Wonderful* in

1982, but both fairly lackluster parts. More promising was a starring role opposite Rodney Dangerfield in the comedy *Easy Money*, before a part alongside De Niro in *Once Upon A Time in America* put him back in *Raging Bull* territory as a tough Italian-American mobster.

This was one of many parts that had the diminutive Pesci as the hard man, sometimes verging on the psychopath, as exemplified (again opposite De Niro) in his Tommy De Vito in *GoodFellas*, for which this time he got to win the Oscar for Best Supporting Actor. Other memorable "baddies" that followed included a terrific performance as co-conspirator David Ferrie in *JFK* (1991), "likeable" con-man Leo Getz in three of the *Lethal Weapon* movies, the bumbling crook Harry Lime in *Home Alone* (1990) and *Home Alone 2: Lost In New York* (1992), and a minor role in De Niro's directorial debut *A Bronx Tale* (1993).

Although the *Home Alone* films were a commercial success, Pesci's excursions into comedy, including 8 *Heads In A Duffel Bag* (1997) and 1997's *Gone Fishin'* (1997), have not always done that well at the box office. The stereotypical "Joe Pesci" role, at its most terrifyingly volatile in Scorsese's *Casino* in 1995, is what he's always been recognized for—a characterization that clearly had a prime starting point in the short-fused Joey La Motta of *Raging Bull*.

### Unfulfilled promise

With even less acting experience than Joe Pesci (who brought her to Scorsese and De Niro's attention), when Cathy Moriarty got the role of Vickie La Motta in *Raging Bull* she'd only ever appeared on stage at high school, which she was still attending at the time. For her part in the movie she achieved an Oscar nomination, two Golden Globe nominations, and a nomination at the British BAFTA awards—a lot to follow through on.

In the event, her next picture *Neighbors* (1981) was something of a disappointment—an amusing enough comedy with John Belushi and Dan Ackroyd that didn't excite either audiences or critics in a big way. But without the accolades that followed *Raging Bull*, she would never have even had the chance to appear in such prestigious company.

Moriarty's career was abruptly put on hold in 1982, after a car accident that necessitated major back surgery and a slow rehabilitation. She made a muted comeback in 1987 with *White Of The Eye*, followed in 1990 by *Burndown*. Both were fairly obscure low-budget pictures, but the actress garnered favorable notices from the satirical comedy *Soapdish* (1991) in her role as an archetypal soap opera diva. She was similarly feted after another parody on American culture, 1993's *Matinee*, in which she played a Fifties heroine of B-movie horror flicks. Then in 1995 the child-oriented *Casper* had Moriarty returning to the camp mode of *Soapdish*, after which she would find more success in television than on the cinema screen. Her television work included a high-profile sit-com lead in the short-lived CBS series *Bless This House*, and a 1995 episode in HBO's *Tales From The Crypt* that earned her a Cable ACE award.

Cathy Moriarty appeared in more than a dozen movies during the latter half of the Nineties, including *Cop Land* with Scorsese favorites Harvey Keitel, Ray Liotta, and her old sparring partner, Robert De Niro. But since she married

Joseph Gentile in 1999, she has focused on their twins (born in 2000), and another daughter born in 2001.

In 2002 (under her married name of Cathy Moriarty-Gentile) she did reunite once again with De Niro in *Analyze That*, a sequel to his 1999 comedy *Analyze This*. However, what with personally running her Beverly Hills pizza restaurant as well as devoting time to her family, Moriarty's acting career seems to be low on her list of priorities. The Hollywood stardom forecast in the wake of her sensational performance in *Raging Bull* seems like it wasn't to be—for the moment, at least.

# following **Raging Bull**

## Scorsese from
## The King Of Comedy **to** Goodfellas

Before embarking on his next film, as soon as *Raging Bull* was released Martin Scorsese used the opportunity to intensify his personal campaign about the problem of color film fading.

Six months before the release, he'd issued a statement saying "Everything we are doing now means nothing!", referring to the fact that, since the early Fifties, when the old three-strip Technicolor ceased to be used by the industry, nearly all color movies were susceptible to rapid fading. There was simply no guarantee that any filmmaker's work shot in color was going to last. Scorsese presented a petition signed by several hundred prestigious names in the film industry to Eastman Kodak—as the main suppliers of film stock worldwide—appealing to Kodak to "recognize its responsibility to the people it services," and "assume a major role in the research and development of a stable color film stock."

Now his major black-and-white film was doing the rounds, making the issue more "topical," Scorsese took advantage of the fact to lecture on the problem at film festivals—including the New York Film Festival—and other industry events. He pointed out the irony that classics made in the Forties were more durable, and proved more reliable to restore, than most films made since. As a result of pressure brought to bear by Scorsese and others, Eastman Kodak have since supplied the industry with stock less likely to fade.

Scorsese and Robert De Niro also went on a European trip to help publicize the release of *Raging Bull*, which was meeting with a mixed reception—particularly in Britain, where the powerful Rank chain of cinemas refused to show it because of its "profane" language. Rank's main competitors, the Grade organization, eventually took the film, but only after some heated exchanges with the film's makers. Marty and Bob, meanwhile, had arrived in London for a gala premier which was subsequently cancelled.

For the next project Scorsese had in mind, he once again saw De Niro playing the lead. Encouraged by the critical if not commercial success of *Raging Bull*, he felt that the actor would be ideal in what would certainly be a highly controversial role—that of Jesus Christ in an adaptation of Nikos Kazantkazi's novel *The Last Temptation Of Christ*. He'd acquired the film rights, Paul Schrader was already working on the script, and Irwin Winkler was set to produce it with finance from Paramount.

De Niro, however, had other ideas—he wanted to make a comedy.

Ten years earlier he'd bought a script by the film critic Paul D. Zimmermann, and—flushed as they both were with the artistic triumph of *Raging Bull*—persuaded Scorsese (as he had with the La Motta biography) that *The King Of Comedy* should be their next film collaboration.

### A life beyond
Set in the "unreal" but utterly familiar world of television, in many ways *The King Of Comedy* is the complete antithesis of

*Raging Bull*. Like Jake La Motta, the central character Rupert Pupkin (played by De Niro) wants to make it at any price, but the similarity ends there. Whereas La Motta's stance is essentially antisocial, driven by guilt-ridden self-doubt and expressed in anger at those around him, ambitious stand-up comedian Pupkin is the absolute opposite. He aspires to the (albeit shallow) values of the media-based society he finds himself in, is blandly but supremely confident of his own ability to succeed, and seemingly all-inclusive in his willingness to please in order to achieve his goal.

With such guiltless ambition, however, comes a ruthless streak. Ostensibly a great fan of talk show host Jerry Langford (Jerry Lewis), he "stalks" the television star in the hope of getting a spot on his program—first by pestering him with a tape he's made of a mock-up "appearance" on the show, then by turning up uninvited at his home. Here we see that Rupert is not simply driven by a naïve determination, however, as he pretends that he and Jerry are old friends in order to impress his new girlfriend Rita.

Unwilling to take no for an answer, with the aid of an equally obsessed female fan, Rupert kidnaps the celebrity, demanding that he gets to appear on the show, which must be broadcast before Jerry is released. The fan gets to fulfil her fantasy of spending the night with her idol, while Rupert fulfils his of appearing on Jerry's show. He's subsequently arrested, but after two years in jail achieves his ambition of becoming rich and famous when, on his release, he writes a best-selling memoir.

The original Zimmermann script had a more ambiguous ending, with Rupert appearing on the Langford show, introduced as "the kidnapping king of comedy" and wowing the studio audience. But we never see that audience, and for all we know this is another contrived "appearance" put together by Pupkin in his basement studio where he shot the first demo tape. De Niro and Scorsese decided that this was perhaps too ambivalent a way to round off the movie, and hastily came up with the happy-ever-after ending which was as deliberately schlocky as the vacuous aspiration that drove Rupert Pupkin.

For De Niro the role of Pupkin entailed a far more radical change of character from Jake La Motta than if he'd taken on the guilt-ridden Christ of *Last Temptation Of Christ*. Here was a man who had no self-doubts about his motives, his ability, or even his decidedly tasteless appearance. As usual, the actor threw himself into the part completely, checking out stand-up comics and—more appropriately—the star-struck wannabes who hung around stage doors and shopped in show-biz memorabilia stores. He soon had the look he wanted, a polkadot jacket, blue shirt, red tie, and white shoes, topped off with *that* moustache. "It was the moustache that told you everything you wanted to know," wrote *Guardian* critic Mark Morris. "The moment you saw the thing on Rupert Pupkin's upper lip, you knew he was a man who thought he was funny but wasn't."

Notwithstanding his declining the *Last Temptation* part (a film Scorsese would make later in the decade), De Niro was very much the driving force at this stage in the director's movie-making. They had come to the notice of the public together, in *Mean Streets* then *Taxi Driver*, but of late, with the box-office failure of both *New York, New York* and *Raging Bull*, it was De Niro who was getting all the high-profile plaudits, with an Oscar nomination for *The Deer Hunter* and Best Actor award for *Raging Bull*.

As far as Scorsese was concerned *The King Of Comedy* marked the point in his career where he realized there was life after *Raging Bull*. Initially, he had vowed that the La Motta saga would be his last picture: "I really thought that was the last movie I was going to make. I thought I was going to go and do documentaries in Rome based on the lives of the saints …" But the creative dynamic that went into *Raging Bull* didn't dissipate once the movie was finished—"I still kept going, but I had no place else to go."

*The King Of Comedy* opened in America in February 1983, but failed to make the impression at the box office that was hoped for, despite the potent duo of De Niro and funny man Jerry Lewis, who was something of an American show-business institution. It was premiered at the Cannes Film Festival, and in Britain received five BAFTA nominations (the UK equivalent of the Academy Awards) despite being a commercial flop and being relegated to British television by the end of the year. Scorsese, and many others, felt that De Niro delivered a superlative performance as the embarrassing Pupkin: "I felt it was De Niro's best performance ever. *The King Of Comedy* was right on the edge for us; we couldn't go any further at that time."

Indeed, Scorsese and De Niro wouldn't work together again until the end of the decade, when *Goodfellas* would be the final movie in Scorsese's so-called "Italian-American" trilogy, of which the second, *Raging Bull*, was widely regarded as their finest collaborative achievement.

## After Hours

Martin Scorsese, meanwhile, would release three films as director before teaming up with Robert De Niro again, including *The Last Temptation of Christ* which he turned his attention to once again as soon as *The King Of Comedy* was released.

Paul Schrader had completed a script from Kazantzaki's novel of *The Last Temptation*, and early in 1983 Paramount told Scorsese they wanted to go ahead with the film. Irwin Winkler and Bob Chartoff—who'd produced *New York, New York* and *Raging Bull*—were on board, and Scorsese spent the next nine months casting and checking out locations, eventually settling on Israel.

This in itself made the studio nervous—they felt in control if a movie was being made in California, or Mexico, or Canada, or even Europe—but the Middle East! Not to mention that the budget began to escalate accordingly, as did Scorsese's proposed schedule. One thing led to another, and when the religious lobby stepped in, putting pressure on Gulf and Western (who owned Paramount) that they should have nothing to do with what they expected to be a blasphemous movie, the studio really started to have second thoughts. By the end of the year they had pulled out, *The Last Temptation Of Christ* was on hold, and Scorsese was looking for another picture to make.

So Scorsese's next movie, rather than the $12 million biblical drama he had planned, was a modestly budgeted "indie" picture in which he had no interference by a big company, a freedom that he'd enjoyed ten years earlier with *Taxi Driver*. From a script by Joe Minion, *After Hours*—set in

Scorsese's favorite stomping ground of Manhattan—is a quirky, Kafkaesque piece covering one disturbing night in the life of an otherwise "normal" guy. He's Paul (played by Griffin Dunne), a computer operator who chances upon an attractive girl in a coffee shop (Rosanna Arquette) who invites him back to her loft apartment in trendy SoHo. The promise of a sexual encounter goes nightmarishly wrong, however, as he soon finds himself alone, with no cash to get home, subject to a series of encounters that get worse as they get more bizarre. The paranoia builds as everyone and every situation seems to be conspiring to stop him escaping the streets, or even surviving the night. Come the dawn, he eventually gets himself smuggled back into the office where he works by "disguising" himself as a piece of sculpture.

Released in 1985, the ninety-six-minute black comedy would come in at just $4.5 million, and go on to gross more than $10 million, with Scorsese winning the Palme d'Or for Best Director at the Cannes Film Festival. The low-key success of *After Hours*, in both commercial and artistic terms, was something of a fillip for Scorsese—none of his previous three narrative movies had scored at the box office, regardless of how they were rated by the critics.

**Intermission**

The revival of his fortunes in the wake of *After Hours* was confirmed with two side projects in 1985 that preceded Scorsese's next major movie, both involving subjects close to his heart. First there was a twenty-four-minute episode in a Steven Spielberg-produced television series "Amazing Stories." The Scorsese film, *Mirror, Mirror*, which he made in just six days and was allowed no final cut, was written by Spielberg and scripted by *After Hours* writer Joseph Minion. It involved Sam Waterston as Jordan, a horror novelist who, though denying he gets scared about such things, begins to see a phantom in the mirror. Charting the nervous breakdown and eventual suicide that ensues, Scorsese pays homage to one of his great cinematic passions (of which he had many), old horror movies. Talking about *Mirror, Mirror,* he cited British Hammer films as a particular influence from his teenage movie-going in the Fifties.

The other labor of love was an acting part, as a club manager in Bertrand Tavernier's Paris-set tribute to the great jazz musicians of the be-bop era, *Round Midnight*. Scorsese had done minor parts before, of course—like the hardly visible stage hand in the final minute of *Raging Bull*, and a creepy passenger in *Taxi Driver*—but this was something more substantial. Via the high reputation he enjoyed in Europe, particularly among the film-crazy French, he'd met Tavernier a couple of years before when researching locations for *Last Temptation*. The director told him he was perfect for the part—"He's just like you, he's a nice guy, but he's ruthless."

During 1985 a number of film projects were briefly linked with Scorsese's name. There was *Dick Tracy*, subsequently directed by its star and producer Warren Beatty; a Paul Schrader script entitled *Gershwin*; and a documentary-style account of the Mafia in New York, *Wise Guy*. But the proposal that ultimately grabbed his attention came as an invitation from the actor Paul Newman—to direct a sequel to his celebrated 1961 pool-room classic, *The Hustler*.

## Smart money

Revisiting Paul Newman's ex-pool hustler Eddie Felson a quarter-of-a-century later, as he sets up and trains new blood (Tom Cruise) in the racket, *The Color of Money* is ostensibly about cash and its often amoral acquisition. But it's also concerned with what drives the characters therein. Cruise's Vincent is a talented but naïve player who finds it hard to lose as part of the necessary con, while Eddie re-learns his old skill at the table to teach the youngster a lesson in a straight tournament. Eddie beats the youngster, only to discover his protégé has deliberately lost to win a pile of betting money—which he presents to his mentor, reminding him where his real talent lies—in the hustle, not the winning.

Coming at a time when Scorsese's star was now in the ascendance, and featuring big names in Newman and the newly famous Cruise, *The Color of Money* was certainly a "commercial" picture in a way that *Raging Bull* and its predecessors never aspired to be. It was distributed by Disney, who'd invested $10 million in a $13 million budget (and who saw a $50 million return on their money), and even had stellar names from the world of music—including Eric Clapton and Robert Palmer—on the soundtrack.

But for all its marketable gloss, it retained many of the qualities that made *Raging Bull* much more than just a film about a "sport" and its participants. As with the fight sequences in *Raging Bull*, each game of pool is shot in a different way to capture the mood of that particular point in the story. Sometimes we're just looking at Cruise center-frame all the way through, in others the camera moves around table with him. And the pursuit of money itself is the occupational backdrop against which Eddie seeks to redeem himself of his past sins (a familiar trait in Scorsese characters), by eventually attempting to reform the avaricious monsters that he has created in Vincent and his girlfriend Carmen. With its obvious parallels to *Raging Bull*, but in the context of a solidly mainstream picture, *The Color Of Money* (released in 1986) marked a point where Martin Scorsese appeared to be increasingly comfortable working in the popular arena without compromising his art as a movie-maker.

The director's "commercial" side was certainly evident over the next year or so when he made two short adverts for Georgio Armani, a sixteen-minute "dramatized" pop video with Michael Jackson (*Bad*), and a more conventional music video—*Somewhere Down The Crazy River*—featuring his old friend Robbie Robertson. But his next motion picture, which began shooting in October 1987, was firmly in the art-as-controversy area that had been occupied by *Raging Bull*.

It was his long-struggled-for chance to film *The Last Temptation Of Christ*.

## The Last Temptation

Just as Fifties horror movies, old boxing newsreels, and innumerable other visual memories from his childhood and teenage years informed Scorsese's films, so the spectacle of both the Catholic Church and the Hollywood biblical epics that he'd grown up with was in the back of his mind when he at last made *The Last Temptation Of Christ*.

But the film was far from a sand-and-sandals saga in the tradition of *King Of Kings*, *The Robe*, and other religious blockbusters. Despite knowing the controversy it would undoubtedly arouse, he made a picture about Jesus as a flawed man, ridden with guilt like the rest of mankind, but ultimately redeemed by giving in to his own destiny.

As a carpenter, Jesus makes crosses for the Romans for their crucifixions. This is the guilt he carries with him, along with having previously rejected Mary Magdalene's love, after which she became a prostitute. Begging her forgiveness, he goes into the desert to discover what God's purpose is with him. Confronted with the choice between good and evil, he realizes he is the Messiah and preaches a philosophy of love accordingly, ending up crucified at the hands of the Romans who see him as a rebel. On the cross he hallucinates that God has "let him off" his duty as Son of God, allowing him to return to Mary Magdalene, who he marries. Years later when Jesus is on his deathbed, his betrayer Judas reminds him that *he* is the traitor, "Your place was on the cross," after which Jesus returns to the cross and his destiny—having overcome his last temptation, to be an ordinary man without the commitment of being humanity's savior.

Fired by scenes and dialogue that many of them had yet to see—including Jesus making love to Mary Magdalene—the religious establishment of most Christian faiths staged vehement protests against the film on its release in 1988, garnering more publicity for it than an avowedly "art house" film would otherwise attract. After the $12 million budget intended to make the film in Israel back in 1983, the film was made with a more constrained spend of $7 million in Morocco, and managed to break just a little above even.

Despite its subject matter, at its core *The Last Temptation Of Christ* has much in common with *Raging Bull*. It's the struggle between the flesh and the spirit, between good and evil, in one man. Jesus finds his eventual self-realization on the cross, Jake La Motta in his "confessional" stage monologues. But much nearer to *Raging Bull* in both setting and characterization would be the third of the "Italian-American" trilogy of New York stories which appeared in 1990—*Goodfellas*.

## A New York story

Before he embarked on *Goodfellas*, Scorsese was involved in another work set in New York City—not in the tough neighborhoods of the Italian-American community he'd grown up in, but, like *After Hours*, in the now-trendy artist loft area of SoHo.

Called *Life Lessons*, it was part of *New York Stories*, a three-film compilation put together by Woody Allen. Along with short works by Allen and Francis Ford Coppola, Scorsese's forty-four-minute piece centers on an artist (played by Nick Nolte) who claims he has "painter's block" when his muse and lover (Rosanna Arquette) leaves for another man. The tension between the two, one a successful artist and the other up-and-coming, is reminiscent of the clash of seemingly compatible personalities (both being in music) in *New York, New York*.

1990's *Goodfellas* was based on the true-life account of gangster Henry Hill by Nick Pileggi, which Scorsese had been considering before he embarked on *The Color of Money*. Compared to Coppola's first two *Godfather* films, which had become something of a yardstick for "Mafia" movies, the film focused on organized crime in the Italian-American community at an essentially more realistic neighborhood level. The world of Robert De Niro's Jimmy Conway, Ray Liotta's Henry Hill and Joe Pesci's Tommy De Vito have more in common with the local hoods of *Mean Streets* and *Raging Bull* than the underworld aristocracy of the Corleone dynasty.

In fact the main protagonists, Hill and Conway, are Irish-Americans who have grown up in an Italian neighborhood, a fact which implies that anybody seduced by the apparent glamor can be part of the Mob life. "As far back as I can remember, I always wanted to be a gangster," Henry's voice-over tells us at the opening of the film. There's no attempt to hide the fact that the organized crime has to do with anything but pure greed for money and the social status it confers. These "wise guys" are ordinary guys, but who nevertheless lead an extraordinary existence outside the moral and behavioral standards of regular society. The juxtaposition of their bizarre world and "normality" is best illustrated when they gather round the table as Tommy's mother (played by Scorsese's mother Catherine) makes them a meal, unaware that they're in the middle of disposing of a body that's in the boot of the car outside.

This relationship with conventional society is interdependent, of course; while a psychopath like Pesci's Tommy can kill with shocking ease, those who benefit most from the criminality are the ones like Henry to whom the power of the Mob opens doors hitherto closed to them. There's a marvelous single steady-cam shot of Henry impressing his girlfriend by taking her into the Copacabana club via the back door, winding through the kitchens and to a place right in front of the stage, where a table is produced as if by magic just as they arrive. Like La Motta's entry into the boxing arena in the similar sequence in *Raging Bull*, it captures the frisson of power when these men connect with the world "out there" on *their* terms.

Costing $25 million, *Goodfellas* was Scorsese's most expensive film to date, though it was still a modest budget by Hollywood standards. It made $50 million just at the US box office, Scorsese's biggest commercial success since *The Color of Money*. But it also signaled a watershed in the director's filmmaking in more fundamental ways.

## Turning point

In many respects *Raging Bull* could have been said to be an impossible act to follow on the part of Martin Scorsese. The very fact that he seriously felt it might be his last feature film bears testament to that. But the energy and dynamism sparked by such an artistic *tour de force* stimulated rather than exhausted his creative resources, which were then channeled into very diverse projects. Though very different pictures, *The King Of Comedy*, *After Hours*, *The Color Of Money*, and *The Last Temptation Of Christ* were all successful on a number of levels, as was *Goodfellas*, described by one writer as "The definitive exploration of the gangster lifestyle."

But although it completed the "Italian-American" trilogy, it marked a turning point in Scorsese's approach. Up until then, his movies had a strongly "spiritual" aspect in that they focused on the inner tensions of his characters, often expressed through issues of guilt and redemption. "I seem to have been drawn to characters and themes which have a sense of religious quest" he would say, calling *Taxi Driver* "extremely religious." Even the guiltless Rupert Pupkin in *The King Of Comedy* is striving for a form of redemption through the recognition that fame will bring, though whether it will make him a "better" person is another question.

At the end of *Goodfellas*, however, there is no redemption for Henry Hill. Having informed on his friends (the "right" moral choice in society's eyes) he feels nothing but self-contempt. He never shared society's values of right and wrong, and the status he enjoyed as a result of crime is not forthcoming, living under a witness protection program—"the life of a schnook," as he puts it.

Having explored through his films issues about personal guilt and responsibility born in part out of his own Catholic upbringing, from here on in Scorsese would approach subjects more "objectively," though still always preoccupied with the complexity and tensions driving his characters. And he would demonstrate, in film after film, that he had simply become an absolute master of his craft—though that mastery would never eclipse the continuing impact of *Raging Bull*, the finest achievement of the period that came to a close with *Goodfellas*.

# aftermath

## Echoes of Raging Bull

In 2005, Halliwell's (responsible for the indispensable *Halliwell's Film Guide* and *Filmgoer's Companion*) announced their list of the 1,000 greatest films of all time. There were three movies by Martin Scorsese in the top 100—*GoodFellas* at number 36, *Taxi Driver* at 13, and *Raging Bull* in seventh place.

Although Halliwell's is not the definitive judge of such matters by any means, and any list like this is both arbitrary and some would say pointless, what is interesting is that all three entries were from that first period of the director's output which *GoodFellas* marked an end to. For, although Scorsese has continued to make memorable and highly distinguished motion pictures in the decade-and-a-half since, it's the films from the earlier part of his career—with *Raging Bull* significant among them—that have had the biggest influence on contemporary cinema.

### Into the mainstream

Not that a change of approach on Scorsese's part always meant a "softening" of either content or characterizations, as his next film after *GoodFellas* would confirm. Released in 1991, the remake of the J. Lee Thompson's 1961 psycho-thriller *Cape Fear* had Robert De Niro in completely over-the-top nasty mode—"a pantomime villain version of Travis Bickle," to quote film writer Geoffrey Macnab. And likewise in 1995's

*Casino*, with De Niro and Pesci (the last time either actor has worked with Scorsese to date) again the ruthlessly violent mobsters, set in the gambling mecca of Las Vegas.

Possibly Martin Scorsese's most talked-about film of recent years, the epic *Gangs Of New York* (2002), was the subject of controversy even before it was released because of the amount of blood-letting that the director saw as essential to the story; it was an identical debate to that which erupted when *Raging Bull* first appeared in 1980. Set in the early days of the city, when Irish gangs waged a violent war against each other for control of the streets, the saga had taken four years just to get into production. Eventually the budget of $97 million (the biggest in Scorsese's career) was raised, and the film went on to make $190 worldwide at the box office before the release of DVD, video, and television rights. It went on to garner ten Oscar nominations, and Scorsese won the Best Director award at the Golden Globes.

In production at the time of writing, Martin Scorsese's next motion picture, *The Departed*, concerns an Irish "mafia" infiltrating the Boston police force and vice versa. Due for release in 2006, it promises to be another film that pulls no more punches than did *Raging Bull* a quarter-of-a-century before.

During these latter years, Scorsese's canon of work has been equally characterized by less turbulent themes. In 1993 he took many by surprise with the elegantly shot romantic costume drama, *The Age Of Innocence*. Then, in 1997 came *Kundun*, a film addressing the Chinese invasion of Tibet in which the serenity of the deposed Dalai Lama is emphasized rather than the camera dwelling on the slaughter that accompanied his fall.

With Nicholas Cage as its passive but compassionate central character, *Bringing Out The Dead* (1999) was the study of a paramedic suffering the anguish of sometimes failing to save a life. And in 2004, Scorsese tackled the internal anguish of one man against a far broader backdrop, when he completed his epic film about Hollywood giant Howard Hughes, *The Aviator*.

Starring Leonardo DiCaprio (who, via *Gangs Of New York* and the upcoming *The Departed* would appear in three consecutive Scorsese films), the story of the legendary film producer and airplane manufacturer was a "natural" subject for Scorsese. It concerned the inner conflicts of a complex and "difficult" individual, but played out in the star-studded context of the early days of movie-making. In fact, *The Aviator* bears many similarities to *Raging Bull*. The central character seeks his personal fulfilment in success in the public arena— in Hughes's case it's making movies, in La Motta's the fight game. Both are high-profile pursuits where the prize for winning is not just money but social status and all that comes with it. In the case of the movie mogul, that means the company of the most beautiful actresses in Hollywood, for the boxing champ it's the only chance he'll ever get to be with a woman as desirable as Vickie.

Both men are plagued by guilt and insecurity, exacerbated by their ruthless pursuit of their ambitions—conflicts of the soul that eventually bring about their individual downfalls. Jake La Motta seeks solace and redemption in his nightly stage confessional, finally recognizing he is alone as he addresses himself in the mirror. Howard Hughes, once a man of power and influence, retreats into the solitary confinement of a recluse, driven by a fanatical ascetism in order to purge himself of the "impurities" (that is, his own transgressions) of the outside world.

## Reference point

While Scorsese had taken his place in the movie-making mainstream over the fifteen years since *GoodFellas*, the enduring influence his filmmaking would have on younger directors came in the main from the body of work that preceded it. A resurgence of independent cinema in the Nineties, similar to the "movie brat" revolution which shook up Hollywood in the Seventies (and which Scorsese was a part of), saw new directors coming through to whom the Scorsese of the "Italian-American" period was almost a father figure.

The harsh reality evoked by his focus on antiheroes, the pioneering of authentic dialogue as a device to reveal more about a character than just the message of the words themselves, the documentary style of the actual story-telling; these were elements in Scorsese's pictures which would become creative reference points for Quentin Tarantino, Paul Thomas Anderson, Michael Mann, and others.

The first impact of Scorsese's "Italian-American" films was actually seen earlier, in documentary-style films of the early Eighties such as William Friedkin's *Cruising* (1980), and Daniel Petrie's *Fort Apache: The Bronx* (1980), both of which came over as refreshingly realistic in their characterizations.

On the matter of the dialogue, this was never more in evidence than in *Raging Bull*. Just as the screenplay in a Tarantino or Kevin Smith film is startlingly "authentic" with its pop-culture references and textuality, so the script in *Raging Bull* does the same in the context of Forties working class popular culture, set in a time when people "went out" a lot more, and when television didn't dominate their lives.

Scorsese might ask us to "care" about Jake La Motta a lot more than, for instance, Tarantino invites sympathy for his protagonists in 1994's *Pulp Fiction*, but the film is essentially non-judgmental—any "judgment" is left for Jake himself to arrive at. And even though *Pulp Fiction*, as its title implies, is driven by a deliberately "trash" aesthetic compared to Scorsese's more authoritative work, the casual violence and profane language of its perpetrators echoes much that we see in the "Italian-American" films, particular in the characters played by Joe Pesci.

Paul Thomas Anderson was only ten years old when *Raging Bull* was released. He's one of the most accomplished of the new breed of "VCR filmmakers" (Tarantino is another), so-called because through seeing thousands of films on video they have an encyclopedic knowledge of technique and cultural references.

Anderson cites Scorsese as a key influence, and it's clearly evident in his handful of highly crafted films. His movies (typically *Sydney* in 1996 and 1999's *Magnolia*) are characterized by his use of ensemble casts and complex storylines, often dealing with family relationships, especially fathers and their children. Stylistically, he's indebted to Scorsese in what is something of a personal trademark—his use of very few cuts and heavy reliance on tracking shots. The famous boxing arena steady-cam shot in *Raging Bull* was clearly an inspiration in Anderson's most commercially successful film *Boogie Nights* (1997), which opens with a three-minute tracking shot without a single cut.

Michael Mann is best known for gritty crime dramas, his reputation being cemented with *Thief* in 1981 and *Manhunter* (1986), in both of which he created highly atmospheric environments in which the characters were explored through thought-provoking yet highly realistic dialogue. It was the use of hard-edged realism as a backdrop to often complex psychological drama that harked back directly to the way that Scorsese and De Niro approached the Jake La Motta character in *Raging Bull*.

Mann's most celebrated action thriller was *Heat* (1995), the memorable first pairing of De Niro with Al Pacino in which the former's ruthless armed robber comes to terms with a growing respect for his foe, Pacino's streetwise but world-weary cop. At the end of the film it's clear that what the two have in common is far greater than what divides them. Written by Mann, it's a storyline that could well have made a Scorsese film a few years earlier.

But the Michael Mann film which invites closest comparison to *Raging Bull* in terms of subject matter is *Ali*, the ambitious 2001 biopic of the boxing legend (sensationally played by Will Smith). More in the grand tradition of Oliver Stone (*The Doors, JFK, Nixon*) or Richard Attenborough (*Ghandi, Chaplin*), the epic treatment tells a heroic story while avoiding too deep an analysis of what makes the central characters tick. Quite the opposite to *Raging Bull*, where the actual detail of La Motta's boxing history (though graphically evoked) is passed over in favor of a study of his complex and troubled psyche.

And similarly comparing *Raging Bull* to other "boxing movies" that have appeared since, from the *Rocky* sequels in the Eighties (*Rocky III* and *IV*) to 2005's *Cinderella Man*, tells us something about the Scorsese film's basic *raison d'etre*—it's actually not a fight film as such.

The *Rocky* films conformed to the classic "fight film" formula of a fictional drama where boxing was central to its creation, the story and characterizations of the film simply couldn't have been developed in any other context. A recent excursion in this genre was Ron Howard's *Cinderella Man* (2005), based on the true story of a Depression-hit ex-prizefighter who returns to the ring to save his family from destitution.

Then there are boxing pictures that attempt a purely biographical/quasi-factual approach, traditionally films like *Somebody Up There Likes Me* (1956) that were based on the careers of famous champs. As well as *Ali*, latterly we've seen Hurricane Carter (Denzel Washington in *Hurricane*, 1999) celebrated in this way.

In recent years there have been a few "fight films" similar to *Raging Bull* in intent—where boxing is the background against which the core issues of the movie are addressed. These have included the under-rated *Spike Of Bensonhurst*, Paul Morrisey's 1988 tale of an aspiring Italian-American boxer who gets involved with a Mafia boss's daughter, and, in 2004, Clint Eastwood's Academy Award-winning *Million Dollar Baby*.

The Eastwood film won the Award for both Best Film and Best Director, categories in which Martin Scorsese was nominated that same year for *The Aviator*. Once again, the Oscar would prove elusive to Scorsese, despite a now-acknowledged track record as one of, if not *the*, most important film artists of modern times. But his is a reputation founded on firmer ground than mere accolades, though recognition by the Academy would have seemed appropriate if not inevitable by now.

Martin Scorsese's standing as a giant of the cinema has been based on a consistently uncompromizing faith in what he is doing.

In the making of *Raging Bull* this was particularly apparent. Where at first he had doubts about the project for a number of reasons, once committed to it he became obsessed with every last detail of its execution. His emotional involvement was such that Scorsese was convinced at the time that this would be the last movie he'd make.

But the energy he poured into it couldn't simply be turned off when he'd finished; the film instead became a turning point and creative catalyst in a career that still flourishes twenty-five years later. In that respect, *Raging Bull* stands as a monument not just to the technical brilliance, but to the artistic tenacity, of its creator.

# appendix 1

## The Music Of *Raging Bull*

As in many of Martin Scorsese's movies, before and after, *Raging Bull* is full of what are known as "needle drops"—records (or more often clips of records) that represent the world that the movie is set in, the aural backdrop to the society its characters inhabit. More often than not there's a "realistic" rationale for a particular item on the soundtrack; it's coming out of a jukebox in a bar, or on the radio in a domestic scene, or playing in the background at a nightclub. In fact, one of Scorsese's major innovations was making the "score" of his films an eclectic mix of evocative sounds from the period, and it is an approach that has been adopted by many contemporary filmmakers since—particularly cutting-edge directors like Quentin Tarantino, David Lynch, Michael Mann, etc.

"When you think of moments from your own life, you remember feelings and the way that different sights and sounds and textures connect to those feelings," Scorsese would write in the liner notes to a CD release of the *Raging Bull* soundtrack. "For all of us, the places we grew up and the feelings we experienced within those places remain inseparable." He clearly recognizes that the sounds around us are as much a part of the fabric of our lives as what we actually see, so to him as a filmmaker they are of equal importance as the background details of décor, fashion, or whatever. Just as a street scene has to feature the right cars of the period, or a shot of the family kitchen include the authentic food products of the day, so the radio has to be playing the typical tunes.

But it doesn't stop there. In making that choice, Scorsese also considers pieces of music on the basis of how they reflect the mood of a particular scene. So while Vickie La Motta waits outside the nightclub while her husband carries on carousing inside, we hear a doo-wop record playing in the background— "I miss you so much, please come home" is the repeated plea on the chorus of The Hearts' "Lonely Nights."

Anyone who thinks that picking the music specific to that one period, the late Forties and early Fifties, was likely to narrow Scorsese's choice was wrong. There's a huge variety here; big band tracks abound (Artie Shaw, Benny Goodman, Gene Krupa, and Harry James are all to be heard), there are vocal groups from the jazzy Ink Spots to the doo-wop of The Hearts, and crooners that include Frank Sinatra ("Come Fly With Me"), Tony Bennett with "Blue Velvet," and Bing Crosby singing "One More Chance." Nat King Cole's wonderfully smooth "Mona Lisa" is in there, there's a snatch of Marilyn Monroe with "Bye, Bye, Baby," and Louis Prima and Keely Smith on the classic double "Just a Gigolo/I Ain't Got Nobody" typify small-band jump-jive music of the era.

Italian and Latin music was hugely popular during that time, particularly in the Italian-American community, so we have Renato Carosone's "Scapricciatiella" ("Infatuation"), Orazio Strano's "Turi Giuliano," and Patricio Teixeira's "Nao Tenho Lagrimas," plus "Stornelli Fiorentini" and "Vivere," both by Carlo Buti.

And, most spectacularly in the way in which it ties in with the images, there's the theme music (not emanating from a "natural source" but in the fashion of normal soundtrack music), that accompanies the opening iconic sequence of Jake La Motta shadow boxing alone in the ring in his hooded leopard-skin robe. It's the Intermezzo from the opera *Cavalleria Rusticana* by the nineteenth-century Italian composer Pietro Mascagni. Two other items by Mascagni are featured in the film, "Barcarolle" from *Silvano* and the Intermezzo from *Guglielmo Ratcliff*. There are also three pieces in the movie by Robbie Robertson, who collaborated with Martin Scorsese in putting together the soundtrack music.

## Music featured in the film

Cavalleria Rusticana: Intermezzo (Mascagni) – Orchestra of Bologna Municop Thetra, Conductor Arturo Basile

Jersey Bounce (1942) – Benny Goodman & His Orchestra

Prisoner Of Love (1934) – Russ Columbo & Nat Shilkret's Orchestra

Just One More Chance (1931) – Bing Crosby with Victor Young's Orchestra

Cow-Cow Boogie (1941) – Ella Fitzgerald featuring The Ink Spots

Vivere – Carlo Buti

Whispering Grass (Don't Tell The Trees) (1940) – The Ink Spots

Two O'clock Jump (1939) – Harry James & His Orchestra

Drum Boogie (1941) – Gene Krupa & His Orchestra

All Or Nothing At All (1940) – Harry James & His Orchestra featuring Frank Sinatra

Flash (1939) – Harry James & His Orchestra

My Reverie (1939) – Larry Clinton & His Orchestra

Stornelli Fiorentini – Carol Buti

Webster Hall – Robbie Robertson

Big Noise From Winnetka (1938) – Bob Crosby & The Bobcats

Frenesi (1940) – Artie Shaw & His Orchestra

Do I Worry? (1940) – The Ink Spots

Turi Guiliano – Orazio Strano

Silvano: Barcarolle (Mascagni) – Orchestra of Bologna Municop Thetra, Conductor Arturo Basile

Stone Cold Dead In The Market (1946) – Ella Fitzgerald & Louis Jordan

Nao Tenho Lagrimas (1937) – Patricio Teixeira

Heartaches (1947) – Ted Weems

Guglielmo Ratcliff: Intermezzo (Mascagni) – Orchestra of Bologna Municop Thetra, Conductor Arturo Basile

At Last – Robbie Robertson

A New Kind Of Love – Robbie Robertson

Till Then (1944) – The Mills Brothers

Mona Lisa (1950) – Nat King Cole

That's My Desire (1947) – Frankie Laine

Bye, Bye, Baby (1953) – Marilyn Monroe

Blue Velvet (1951) – Tony Bennett

Night Train – Robbie Robertson

Scapricciatiello (Infatuation) (1956) – Renato Carosone

Come Fly With Me (1957) – Frank Sinatra

Just A Gigolo/I Ain't Got Nobody (1956) – Louis Prima & Keely Smith

Lonely Nights (1955) – The Hearts

Tell The Truth (1956) – Ray Charles

Prisoner Of Love (1946) – Perry Como

Cavalleria Rusticana: Intermezzo (Mascagni) (Reprise) – Orchestra of Bologna Municop Thetra, Conductor Arturo Basile

*Raging Bull: The Original Soundtrack* is available as a double-CD on the Capitol label in the United States (ASIN no. B0009X75AQ) and EMI in the United Kingdom (Cat no. 7243560322)

# appendix 2

**Martin Scorsese Filmography**

The Departed (2006) (filming)
No Direction Home (documentary)
The Aviator (2004)
Feel Like Going Home (2003) (documentary, episode of "The Blues" TV series)
Gangs Of New York (2002)
Bringing Out The Dead (1999)
My Voyage To Italy (1999) (documentary)
Kundun (1997)
A Personal Journey With Martin Scorsese Through American Movies (1995) (documentary)
Casino (1995)
The Age Of Innocence (1993)
Cape Fear (1991)
Goodfellas (1990)
Made In Milan (1990) (documentary)
New York Stories (1989) (segment of "Life Lessons")
The Last Temptation Of Christ (1988)
Bad (1987)
The Color of Money (1986)
After Hours (1985)
The King Of Comedy (1983)
Raging Bull (1980)
The Last Waltz (1978)

New York, New York (1977)

Taxi Driver (1976)

Alice Doesn't Live Here Anymore (1974)

Italianamerican (1974) (documentary)

Mean Streets (1973)

Boxcar Bertha (1972)

Street Scenes 1970 (1970) (documentary)

Who's That Knocking At My Door? (1967)

The Big Shave (1967)

It's Not Just You, Murray! (1964)

What's a Nice Girl Like You Doing In A Place Like This? (1963)

Vesuvius VI (1959) (early amateur film)

# appendix 3

**Robert De Niro Filmography**

Hide And Seek (2005)

The Bridge Of San Luis Rey (2004)

Meet The Fockers (2004)

Shark Tale (voice) (2004)

Godsend (2004)

Analyze That (2002)

City By The Sea (2002)

Showtime (2002)

The Score (2001)

Fifteen Minutes (2001)

Meet The Parents (2000)

Men Of Honor (2000)

The Adventures Of Rocky & Bullwinkle (2000)

Flawless (1999)

Analyze This (1998)

Ronin (1998)

Cop Land (1997)

Great Expectations (1997)

Jackie Brown (1997)

Wag The Dog (1997)

The Fan (1996)

Marvin's Room (1996)

Sleepers (1996)

Casino (1995)

Heat (1995)

Les Cent Et Une Nuits (1995)

Mary Shelley's Frankenstein (1994)

A Bronx Tale (1993)

Mad Dog And Glory (1993)

This Boy's Life (1993)

Night And The City (1992)

Backdraft (1991)

Cape Fear (1991)

Guilty By Suspicion (1991)

Mistress (1991)

Awakenings (1990)

Goodfellas (1990)

Stanley And Iris (1990)

Jackknife (1989)

We're No Angels (1989)

Midnight Run (1988)

Angel Heart (1987)

The Untouchables (1987)

The Mission (1986)

Brazil (1985)

Falling In Love (1984)

Once Upon A Time In America (1984)

King Of Comedy (1982)

True Confessions (1981)

Raging Bull (1980)

The Deer Hunter (1978)

New York, New York (1977)

The Last Tycoon (1976)

1900 (1976)

Taxi Driver (1976)

The Godfather Part 2 (1974)

Bang The Drum Slowly (1973)

Mean Streets (1973)

The Gang That Couldn't Shoot Straight (1971)

Jennifer On My Mind (1971)

Born To Win (1971)

The Swap (1971)

Bloody Mama (1970)

Hi, Mom! (1970)

The Wedding Party (1969)

Greetings (1968)

Three Rooms In Manhattan (1965)

# appendix 4

**Joe Pesci Filmography**

The Good Shepherd (2006) *(filming)*
Lethal Weapon 4 (1998)
Gone Fishin' (1997)
8 Heads In A Duffel Bag (1997)
Casino (1995)
With Honors (1994)
Jimmy Hollywood (1994)
A Bronx Tale (1993)
Home Alone 2: Lost in New York (1992)
The Public Eye (1992)
Lethal Weapon 3 (1992)
My Cousin Vinny (1992)
JFK (1991)
The Super (1991)
Home Alone (1990)
Goodfellas (1990)
Betsy's Wedding (1990)
Catchfire (1990)
Lethal Weapon 2 (1989)
Moonwalker (1988)
The Legendary Life Of Ernest Hemingway (1988)
Man On Fire (1987)
Eureka (1984)
Once Upon A Time In America (1984)

Tutti Dentro (1984) (Italian, aka Everybody In Jail)
Easy Money (1983)
Smokey And The Bandit Part 3 (1983) (uncredited)
Dear Mr. Wonderful (1982)
I'm Dancing As Fast As I Can (1982)
Raging Bull (1980)
The Death Collector (1976)
Hey, Let's Twist (1961) (uncredited)

# appendix 5

## Cathy Moriarty Filmography

Analyze That (2002)

Prince Of Central Park (2000)

Little Pieces (2000)

Next Stop, Eternity (2000)

But I'm A Cheerleader (1999)

New Waterford Girl (1999)

Crazy In Alabama (1999)

Gloria (1999)

P.U.N.K.S. (1999)

Red Team (1999)

Digging To China (1998)

Hugo Pool (1997)

Cop Land (1997)

Dream With The Fishes (1997)

A Brother's Kiss (1997)

Women Without Implants (1997)

Foxfire (1996)

Casper (1995)

Forget Paris (1995)

Opposite Corners (1995)

Pontiac Moon (1994)

Me And The Kid (1993)

Another Stakeout (1993)

Matinee (1993)

The Gun In Betty Lou's Handbag (1992)
The Mambo Kings (1992)
Soapdish (1991)
Kindergarten Cop (1990)
Burndown (1990)
White Of The Eye (1987)
Neighbors (1981)
Raging Bull (1980)

# appendix 6

Full Cast and Crew of Raging Bull

**Directed by**
Martin Scorsese

**Writing credits**

| | | |
|---|---|---|
| Jake La Motta | .... | (book) (as Jake La Motta) |
| and Joseph Carter | .... | (book) |
| and Peter Savage | .... | (book) |
| Paul Schrader | .... | (screenplay) |
| and Mardik Martin | .... | (screenplay) |

**Cast** (in credits order)

| | | |
|---|---|---|
| Robert De Niro | .... | Jake La Motta |
| Cathy Moriarty | .... | Vickie Thailer La Motta |
| Joe Pesci | .... | Joey La Motta |
| Frank Vincent | .... | Salvy Batts |
| Nicholas Colasanto | .... | Tommy Como |
| Theresa Saldana | .... | Lenore La Motta, Joey's wife |
| Mario Gallo | .... | Mario |
| Frank Adonis | .... | Patsy |
| Joseph Bono | .... | Guido |
| Frank Topham | .... | Toppy |
| Lori Anne Flax | .... | Irma |
| Charles Scorsese | .... | Charlie, man at table with Como |

| | | |
|---|---|---|
| Don Dunphy | .... | Himself/Radio announcer [Dauthuille fight] |
| Bill Hanrahan | .... | Eddie Eagan |
| Rita Bennett | .... | Emma, Miss 48s |
| James V. Christy | .... | Dr. Pinto |
| Bernie Allen | .... | Comedian |
| Floyd Anderson | .... | Jimmy Reeves |
| Gene LeBell | .... | Ring announcer |
| Harold Valan | .... | Referee [Reeves fight] |
| Victor Magnotta | .... | Fighting soldier [Reeves fight] |
| Johnny Barnes | .... | Sugar Ray Robinson |
| John Thomas | .... | Trainer [first Robinson fight] |
| Kenny Davis | .... | Referee [first Robinson fight] |
| Paul Carmello | .... | Ring announcer [first Robinson fight] |
| Jimmy Lennon Sr. | .... | Ring announcer [second Robinson fight] (as Jimmy Lennon) |
| Bobby Rings | .... | Referee [second Robinson fight] |
| Kevin Mahon | .... | Tony Janiro |
| Marty Denkin | .... | Referee [Janiro fight] (as Martin Denkin) |
| Shay Duffin | .... | Ring announcer [Janiro fight] |
| Eddie Mustafa Muhammad | .... | Billy Fox |

| "Sweet" Dick Whittington | .... | Ring announcer [Fox fight] |
| Jack Lotz | .... | Referee [Fox fight] |
| Kevin Breslin | .... | Heckler [Fox fight] |
| Louis Raftis | .... | Marcel Cerdan |
| Frank Shain | .... | Ring announcer [Cerdan fight] |
| Coley Wallace | .... | Joe Louis [Cerdan fight] |
| Fritzie Higgins | .... | Woman with Vickie [Cerdan fight] |
| George Latka | .... | Referee [Cerdan fight] |
| Fred Dennis | .... | Cornerman #1 [Cerdan fight] |
| Robert B. Loring | .... | Cornerman #2 [Cerdan fight] |
| Johnny Turner | .... | Laurent Dauthuille |
| Vern De Paul | .... | Dauthuille's trainer |
| Chuck Bassett | .... | Referee [Dauthuille fight] |
| Ken Richards | .... | Reporter at phone booth [Dauthuille fight] |
| Peter Fain | .... | Dauthuille cornerman [Dauthuille fight] |
| Billy Varga | .... | Ring announcer [third Robinson fight] (as Count Billy Varga) |
| Harvey Parry | .... | Referee [third Robinson fight] |
| Ted Husing | .... | Himself, announcer [third Robinson fight] (voice) (archive footage) |

| | | |
|---|---|---|
| Michael Badalucco | .... | Soda fountain clerk |
| Thomas Beansy | .... | Lobasso Beansy |
| Paul Forrest | .... | Monsignor |
| Peter Petrella | .... | Johnny |
| Sal Serafino Tomassetti | .... | Webster Hall bouncer |
| Geraldine Smith | .... | Janet |
| Mardik Martin | .... | Copa waiter |
| Maryjane Lauria | .... | Girl #1 |
| Linda Artuso | .... | Girl #2 |
| Peter Savage | .... | Jackie Curtie |
| Daniel P. Conte | .... | Detroit promoter |
| Joe Malanga | .... | Bodyguard |
| Sabine Turco Jr. | .... | Bouncer at Copa |
| Steve Orlando | .... | Bouncer at Copa |
| Silvio García Jr. | .... | Bouncer at Copa |
| John Arceri | .... | Maitre d' |
| Joseph A. Morale | .... | Man at Table #1 |
| James Dimodica | .... | Man at Table #2 |
| Robert Uricola | .... | Man outside cab |
| Andrea Orlando | .... | Woman in cab |
| Allan Malamud | .... | Reporter at Jake's house |
| D.J. Blair | .... | State Atty. Bronson |
| Laura James | .... | Mrs. Bronson |
| Richard McMurray | .... | J.R |
| Mary Albee | .... | Underage ID girl |
| Lisa Katz | .... | Woman with ID girl |
| Candy Moore | .... | Linda |
| Richard A. Berk | .... | Musician #1 |
| Theodore Sauners | .... | Musician #2 |
| Noah Young | .... | Musician #3 |

| Nick Trisko | .... | Carlo, bartender |
| Lou Tiano | .... | Ricky |
| Bob Evan Collins | .... | Arresting deputy #1 |
| Wally K. Berns | .... | Arresting deputy #2 (as Wally Berns) |
| Allen Joseph | .... | Jeweler (as Allan Joseph) |
| Bob Aaron | .... | Prison guard #1 |
| Glenn Leigh Marshall | .... | Prison guard #2 |
| Martin Scorsese | .... | Barbizon stagehand |

Rest of cast listed alphabetically:

| Bruno DiGiorgi | .... | Soda fountain clerk #2 (uncredited) |
| Marty Farrell | .... | Heckler in bar (uncredited) |
| Tony Lip | .... | Patron at nightclub (uncredited) |
| Bill Mazer | .... | Reporter (uncredited) |
| Dennis O'Neill | .... | Dancer (uncredited) |
| John Turturro | .... | Man at table, Webster Hall (uncredited) |
| McKenzie Westmore | .... | Jake's daughter (uncredited) |
| Jimmy Williams | .... | Reporter (uncredited) |

**Produced by**

| Robert Chartoff | .... | producer |
| Hal W. Polaire | .... | associate producer |
| Peter Savage | .... | associate producer |
| Irwin Winkler | .... | producer |

**Non-Original Music by**
Pietro Mascagni
("Intermezzo" from opera "Cavalleria rusticana")

**Cinematography by**
Michael Chapman

**Film Editing by**
Thelma Schoonmaker

**Casting by**
Cis Corman

**Production Design by**
Gene Rudolf        ....     (New York)

**Art Direction by**
Sheldon Haber     ....     (New York)

**Set Decoration by**
Phil Abramson
Frederic C. Weiler (as Fred Weiler)

**Costume Design by**
John Boxer
Richard Bruno

**Makeup Department**
Verne Caruso     ....     hair stylist
Mary Keats     ....     hair stylist

| Mike Maggi | .... | makeup artist |
| Mona Orr | .... | hair stylist |
| Jean Burt Reilly | .... | hair stylist |
| Michael Westmore | .... | makeup designer |
| Allen Payne | .... | hair stylist (uncredited) |

**Production Management**

| James D. Brubaker | .... | production manager |

**Second Unit Director or Assistant Director**

| Henry Bronchtein | .... | DGA trainee |
| Elie Cohn | .... | second assistant director |
| Joan Feinstein | .... | second assistant director |
| Jerry Grandey | .... | first assistant director |
| Allan Wertheim | .... | first assistant director |

**Art Department**

| Terry L. Adams | .... | assistant property master |
| Kirk Axtell | .... | art director: Los Angeles |
| Hank Bauer | .... | chief carpenter |
| Emily Ferry | .... | property master |
| William Lowry | .... | construction grip (as William J. Lowry Sr.) |
| Gene Ludvigsen | .... | construction foreman |
| Alan Manser | .... | art director: Los Angeles |
| Jack Mortellaro | .... | set dresser |
| Eugene Powell | .... | scenic artist |
| Thomas Saccio | .... | property master (as Tom Saccio) |
| Hans Swanson | .... | assistant property master |

| | | |
|---|---|---|
| Louis S. Toth Jr. | .... | head construction grip (as Lou Toth Jr.) |
| Linda Conaway-Parsloe | .... | assistant art director (uncredited) |

## Sound Department

| | | |
|---|---|---|
| Michael Evje | .... | sound mixer |
| Gary S. Gerlich | .... | sound effects editor |
| Walter A. Gest | .... | sound recordist (as Walter Gest) |
| Richard Guinness | .... | boom operator |
| Jim Henrikson | .... | music editor |
| David J. Kimball | .... | sound re-recording engineer |
| Les Lazarowitz | .... | sound mixer |
| Victoria Martin | .... | assistant sound effects editor |
| Donald O. Mitchell | .... | sound re-recording engineer |
| Bill Nicholson | .... | sound re-recording engineer |
| Gary Ritchie | .... | sound recordist |
| Robert Sciretta | .... | cable person |
| Murray Siegel | .... | cable person |
| Chester Slomka | .... | sound effects editor |
| Pat Suraci | .... | boom operator |
| Frank E. Warner | .... | supervising sound effects editor (as Frank Warner) |
| Bill Wylie | .... | sound effects editor (as William J. Wylie) |

## Special Effects by

| | | |
|---|---|---|
| Raymond Klein | .... | special effects |
| Max E. Wood | .... | special effects |

## Stunts

| | | |
|---|---|---|
| Jimmy Nickerson | .... | stunt coordinator (as Jim Nickerson) |
| Steven Burnett | .... | stunts (uncredited) |
| Bennie Moore | .... | stunts (uncredited) |

## Other Crew

| | | |
|---|---|---|
| George Alden | .... | transportation captain |
| Ed Arter | .... | transportation captain (as Edward D. Arter) |
| Tim Athan | .... | production assistant |
| Craig Bassett | .... | assistant editor |
| Donah Bassett | .... | negative cutter |
| Dale Benson | .... | location manager |
| Marion Billings | .... | publicist |
| Dustin Blauvelt | .... | first assistant camera |
| Peter J. Breen | .... | dolly grip |
| Mellissa Bretherton | .... | assistant editor |
| Billy Chartoff | .... | production assistant |
| Lisa Zeno Churgin | .... | assistant editor (as Lisa Churgin) |
| Bud Conley | .... | craft service |
| Robert Connors | .... | best boy electric (as Robert Conners) |
| Christopher Cronyn | .... | location manager (as Chris Cronyn) |

| | | |
|---|---|---|
| Janet Crosby | .... | assistant to producers |
| Jean De Niro | .... | production assistant |
| Lenay Drucker | .... | assistant to associate producers |
| Richard Fee | .... | second assistant camera |
| Jeffrey Friedman | .... | assistant editor (as Jeff Friedman) |
| Henry Fusco | .... | best boy electric |
| Donna Gigliotti | .... | assistant: Mr. Scorsese |
| Tom Gilligan | .... | best boy grip |
| Edward Gold | .... | camera operator (as Eddie Gold) |
| June Rachel Guterman | .... | production assistant (as June Guterman) |
| Brian Hamill | .... | still photographer |
| Jim Henry | .... | black and white timer |
| Mary Hickey | .... | production assistant |
| Rob Hummel | .... | special assistance |
| Lori Imbler | .... | assistant to producers |
| Gail Kaszynski | .... | casting assistant |
| Moira Kelly | .... | production office coordinator |
| Yoshio Kishi | .... | associate editor |
| Jake La Motta | .... | consultant (as Jake La Motta) |
| William Loger | .... | costumer (as Bill Loger) |
| Christine M. Loss | .... | still photographer (as Christine Loss) |
| Bruce MacCallum | .... | second assistant camera (as Bruce McCallum) |

| | | |
|---|---|---|
| Joe R. Marquette Jr. | .... | camera operator (as Joe Marquette) |
| John Mavros | .... | assistant editor |
| Kyle McCarthy | .... | assistant to associate producers |
| Ray Mendez | .... | gaffer |
| Michael R. Miller | .... | assistant editor (as Michael Miller) |
| Robert Miller | .... | key grip |
| Susan E. Morse | .... | associate editor |
| Emmet Murphy | .... | special assistance |
| Gloria Norris | .... | researcher |
| Betty M. Nowell | .... | costumer |
| Tom O'Brien | .... | transportation captain |
| Janice Peroni | .... | production assistant |
| Dan Perri | .... | title designer |
| Barry Ping | .... | best boy grip |
| Sonya Polonsky | .... | first assistant editor |
| Marilyn Putnam | .... | costumer |
| Richard Quinlan | .... | gaffer |
| Ed Quinn | .... | key grip |
| Erik T. Ramberg | .... | associate editor |
| Eddie Ramirez | .... | first assistant camera (as Ed Ramirez) |
| Lydia Resurreccion | .... | production accountant |
| Robbie Robertson | .... | music producer |
| Mark Rubin | .... | production assistant |
| Gene Rudolf | .... | visual consultant: Los Angeles |
| Hannah Scheel | .... | script supervisor |

| | | |
|---|---|---|
| Deborah Schindler | .... | assistant: Mr. Scorsese |
| Steve Schottenfeld | .... | production assistant |
| Mary Scott | .... | assistant editor |
| Meryle Selinger | .... | production accountant (as Meryle Selinger) |
| Al Silvani | .... | boxing technical advisor |
| Dean Skipworth | .... | costumer |
| Shawn Slovo | .... | assistant: Mr. De Niro |
| Donna Smith | .... | production office coordinator |
| Marie Sorell | .... | first aid |
| Helene Spinner | .... | production office coordinator |
| Karen I. Stern | .... | assistant editor (as Karen Stern) |
| David Ticotin | .... | production assistant |
| Rachel Ticotin | .... | production assistant |
| Johanne Todd | .... | assistant: Mr. De Niro |
| Frank Topham | .... | technical advisor |
| George Trirogoff | .... | associate editor |
| Mark Warner | .... | associate editor |
| Andrea E. Weaver | .... | costumer (as Andrea Weaver) |
| Charles Winkler | .... | production assistant |
| Todd Coleman | .... | personal assistant: Mr. De Niro (uncredited) |
| Mark Del Costello | .... | personal assistant: Mr. Scorsese (uncredited) |
| Vincent Donohue | .... | rigging grip (uncredited) |
| Don E. FauntLeRoy | .... | first assistant camera (uncredited) |

| | | |
|---|---|---|
| Joe Kelly | .... | grip (uncredited) |
| Gábor Kövér | .... | assistant camera (uncredited) |
| Michael Neale | .... | location manager (uncredited) |
| Marty Eli Schwartz | .... | location manager (uncredited) |
| Michael E. Uslan | .... | production attorney (uncredited) |

# reference sources

**Chapter One**

Christie, Ian, Thompson, David (ed), *Scorsese on Scorsese*,
Faber, UK, 2003
Dougan, Andy, *Martin Scorsese Close Up*,
Orion, UK, 1997
imdb.com

**Chapter Two**

Burnette, Peter (ed), *Martin Scorsese: Interviews*,
University Press of Mississippi, 1999
Robert de Niro: *New York Times*, 23/11/80
Baxter, John, *De Niro: A Biography*,
Harper Collins, UK, 2003
Sabbage, Lisa, *Boxing Clever*,
Netribution Film Network
Kelly, Mary Pat, *Martin Scorsese: A Journey*,
Thunder's Mouth Press, US, 1991
Christie, Ian, Thompson, David (ed), *Scorsese on Scorsese*,
Faber, UK, 2003
*Raging Bull*, MGM Ultimate Edition DVD, 2005
Biskind, Peter, *Easy Riders, Raging Bulls*,
Bloomsbury, UK, 1998

**Chapter Three**

Chapman, Michael, in Ric Gentry's "Michael Chapman
Captures Raging Bull in Black and White" *Millimeter 9*, 2/81

Kelly, Mary Pat, *Martin Scorsese: A Journey*,
Thunder's Mouth Press, US, 1991
Burnette, Peter (ed), *Martin Scorsese: Interviews*,
University Press of Mississippi, 1999
Christie, Ian, Thompson, David (ed), *Scorsese on Scorsese*,
Faber, UK, 2003
imdb.com

**Chapter Four**
Baxter, John, *De Niro: A Biography*,
Harper Collins, UK, 2003
Dougan, Andy, *Martin Scorsese Close Up*,
Orion, UK, 1997
imdb.com
thespiannet.com

**Chapter Five**
Baxter, John, *De Niro: A Biography*,
Harper Collins, UK, 2003
Kelly, Mary Pat, *Martin Scorsese: A Journey*,
Thunder's Mouth Press, US, 1991
Chapman, Michael, in Ric Gentry's "Michael Chapman
Captures Raging Bull in Black and White" *Millimeter 9*, 2/81
Hayes, Kevin J., *Martin Scorsese's Raging Bull*,
Cambridge University Press, UK 2005
("Visual Absurdity in Raging Bull" by Todd Berliner)
Burnette, Peter (ed), *Martin Scorsese: Interviews*,
University Press of Mississippi, US, 1999
Christie, Ian, Thompson, David (ed), *Scorsese on Scorsese*,
Faber, UK, 2003

*Raging Bull*, MGM Ultimate Edition DVD, 2005
imdb.com

## Chapter Six
*Raging Bull*, MGM 20<sup>th</sup> Anniversay Edition DVD, 2000
*Raging Bull*, MGM Ultimate Edition DVD, 2005

## Chapter Seven
Biskind, Peter, *Easy Riders,Raging Bulls*,
Bloomsbury, UK, 1998
Canby, Vincent, *New York Times*, 14/11/80
Kroll, Jack, *Newsweek*, 14/11/80
*Variety*, 12/11/80
Carroll, Kathleen, *New York Daily News*, 14/11/80
Jenkins, Steve, *Monthly Film Journal*, 12/80
Scott, Jay, *Toronto Globe and Mail*, 15/11/80
*Raging Bull*, MGM 20<sup>th</sup> Anniversay Edition DVD, 2000
*Raging Bull*, MGM Ultimate Edition DVD, 2005

## Chapter Eight
Thomson, David, *The New Biographical Dictionary Of Film*,
Little Brown, UK 2002
Baxter, John, *De Niro: A Biography*,
Harper Collins, UK, 2003
Duncan, Paul, *Martin Scorsese*,
Pocket Essentials, UK, 2004
Dougan, Andy, *Martin Scorsese Close Up*,
Orion, UK, 1997
Walker, John (ed), *Halliwell's Film Guide*,
Harper Collins, UK, 2001

imdb.com

lycos.com

en.wikipedia.org

msn.com

the-numbers.com

## Chapter Nine

Christie, Ian, Thompson, David (ed), *Scorsese on Scorsese*,
Faber, UK, 2003

Biskind, Peter, *Easy Riders, Raging Bulls*,
Bloomsbury, UK, 1998

Baxter, John, *De Niro: A Biography*,
Harper Collins, UK, 2003

Wiener, Thomas, "Martin Scorsese Fights Back,"
*American Film*, 11/80

Dougan, Andy, *Martin Scorsese Close Up*,
Orion, UK, 1997

Duncan, Paul, *Martin Scorsese*,
Pocket Essentials, UK, 2004

## Chapter Ten

Macnab, Geoffrey, *The Making of Taxi Driver*,
Unanimous, UK, 2005

Clarkson, Wensley, *Quentin Tarantino:Shooting From The Hip*,
Piatkus, UK, 1995

Walker, John (ed), *Halliwell's Film Guide*,
Harper Collins, UK, 2001

imdb.com

boxing.about.com

en.wikipedia.org

rogerebert.suntimes.com

ymdb.com

## Appendix 1

Review of *Raging Bull* soundtrack CD by John Metzger,
*The Music Box*, Volume 12, #8, 8/05
Review of *Raging Bull* soundtrack CD by Rafael Ruiz,
soundtrack.net, 8/15/05

# selected bibliography

Baxter, John, *De Niro: A Biography*,
Harper Collins, UK, 2003

Biskind, Peter, *Easy Riders, Raging Bulls*,
Bloomsbury, UK, 1998

Biskind, Peter, *Seeing Is Believing*, Henry Holy, US, 2000

Burnette, Peter (ed), *Martin Scorsese: Interviews*,
University Press of Mississippi, US, 1999

Christie, Ian, Thompson, David (ed), *Scorsese on Scorsese*,
Faber, UK, 2003

Dougan, Andy, *Martin Scorsese Close Up*,
Orion, UK, 1997

Duncan, Paul, *Martin Scorsese*, Pocket Essentials, UK, 2004

Hayes, Kevin J., *Martin Scorsese's Raging Bull*,
Cambridge University Press, UK, 2005

Higham, Charles, Greenberg, Joel, *Hollywood In The Forties*,
Barnes & Co, US, 1968

Hirsch, Foster, *Film Noir: The Dark Side Of The Screen*,
Da Capo, US, 1981

Kelly, Mary Pat, *Martin Scorsese: A Journey*,
Thunder's Mouth Press, US, 1991

La Motta, Jake, *Raging Bull: My Story*,
Da Capo, US, 1997

Silver, Alan, Ursini, James, *Film Noir*,
Taschen, Germany, 2004

Woods, Paul (ed), *Scorsese: A Journey Through the American Psyche*, Plexus, UK, 2005

# index